Learn to Use Pivot Tables in an Hour.

Making Excel Easy.

By Carl Nixon

Copyright.

Learn to Use Pivot Tables in an Hour.

First published in 2017 by Carl Nixon T/A Excel-Expert.com, Tonypandy, South Wales, UK.

This edition first published in 2017 by Carl Nixon carl@excel-expert.com.

www.excel-expert.com

The right of Carl Nixon to be identified as the author of this work has been asserted in accordance with sections 77 and 78 of the Copyright Designs and Patents Act 1988.

All rights reserved. No part of this book may be reproduced in any material form (including photocopying or storing in any medium by electronic means) without written permission of the copyright holder except in accordance with the provisions of the Copyright, Designs and Patents Act 1988. Applications for the copyright holder's written permission to reproduce any part of this publication should be addressed to the publishers.

Try Our Other Books

Available on Amazon or get more details from our website;

www.Excel-Expert.com

Introduction

A pivot table is a very powerful data summarization tool built in to Excel. It allows you to explore your data interactively and to discover much more about your data than you could with a normal spreadsheet.

Pivot tables have been around for almost as long as spreadsheets have been. They were first added to Excel in Excel 5, back in 1994. However, by this time pivot tables had already been around for a good few years and were nothing new. They were first introduced in **Lotus Improv** on the **NeXT** platform back in 1991.

So, if pivot tables have been around so long and they are so powerful, why are they still such a mystery to most people and feared by others?

In less than an hour, this book will demystify pivot tables and teach you how to wield their powers in your business.

This book is designed to be easy to follow, with as many illustrations as possible. It is also accompanied by a downloadable spreadsheet that contains the exercises in this book – see the accompanying spreadsheet section in the introduction for more information.

In this book, you will learn how to;

- Create pivot tables.
- Navigate and query pivot tables.
- Create pivot charts.
- Create interactive tables and charts.
- Use slicers

Once you learn to master pivot tables, you will wonder how you ever managed without them.

In the first chapter of this tutorial we will build a simple pivot table and look at some of the possibilities they offer us.

An Important Note About Dates.

It the US dates are written in the **MM/DD/YYYY** format, which is at odds with the rest of the world that normally writes dates in the **DD/MM/YYYY** format. In this book, we use a universal date format;

YYYY/MM/DD

This is to avoid confusion where possible.

Accompanying Spreadsheet.

A spreadsheet containing all of the example data, from all of the exercises in this book, is available from;

http://excel-expert.com/downloads/

It is free and no sign up is required.

While there, why not sign up for our newsletter and get free Kindle copies of my future books? I have a whole series of Excel books lined up and each of them will be briefly available for FREE at launch – these offers only last for 5 days each, so you have to be really quick!

About the Author

Carl Nixon was first introduced to spreadsheets back in 1991. It was on a Commodore Amiga and was very limited compared to today's Excel. It had very limited rows and columns available and had no programming facilities. It certainly didn't contain things like Pivot Tables or even a fraction of the charting options we have today.

Oh, and it was slow…. Brain crushingly slow.

Since then he has worked through a seemingly endless variety of spreadsheets including Lotus 123 (ask your parents if you have never heard of it) and Excel.

For the last 7 years, he has been a freelance Excel consultant serving companies around the world, including Pepsico, Walmart and General Mills. Prior to that he spent 10 years working as a Systems and Procedures Analyst for one of the UK's largest motor insurance companies. It was a role that meant living and breathing spreadsheets, day in, day out.

During this time, his Excel skills grew and grew and he soon became the company "go to guy" for anything Excel related. Word of his Excel skills soon got out and he also became the go to guy for other companies.

Seeing a gap in the market place Carl investigated what Excel services were available locally. He was shocked to find that, other than basic training services, there was very little available locally and even nationally. So, in 2009 he established Excel-Expert.com to plug this gap.

Within a few weeks of launching he was flying around Europe to help companies of all sizes make the most of Excel. He has helped companies, across all industries, save thousands of hours a year and considerable amounts of money.

Dedicated To.

My grandsons Kaiiden, Leiiland and Lawson, and my life partner in crime Debbie.

Contents.

Introduction 4

Accompanying Spreadsheet. 6

About the Author 7

Dedicated To. 8

1. What is a Pivot Table? 11
    Example Data for Our First Pivot Table. 11
    Step 1 – Creating Our Pivot Table. 12
    Step 2 – Populating Our Pivot Table. 15
    Step 3 – Using Our Pivot Table. 17
    Step 4 – Getting Even More Information from Our Pivot Table. 20
    Step 5 – Adding Another Dimension to Our Pivot Table. 22

2. Grouping Pivot Table Items. 25
    Example Data for Grouping in Our Pivot Tables. 25
    Grouping Text Items in Pivot Tables. 25
    Grouping Items in Pivot Tables by Dates. 30

3. Same Pivot Table, Different Look 39
    Example Data for Our Pivot Table. 39
    Setting Up a Pivot Table. 39

4. Multi-Level Pivot Tables. 45
    Example Data to be Multi-Levelled. 45
    Using Multiple Row Fields. 45
    Using Multiple Values. 47
    Multiple Report Filter Fields. 52

5. Frequency Distribution in Pivot Tables. 56
    Example Data for a Frequency Distribution Pivot Table. 56

    Finding Frequency Distribution Using Pivot Tables. 56

6. Charting with Pivot Charts. **64**

    Example Data for Our Pivot Chart. 64

    Creating A Pivot Chart. 65

    Filtering Our Pivot Chart. 66

7. Slicing Pivot Tables with Slicers **72**

    Example Data for Our Pivot Table Slicers. 72

    Adding A Slicer. 73

    Making Multiple Selections. 76

    Clearing Your Selections. 78

8. Updating Pivot Tables. **79**

    How to Refresh Your Pivot Table. 79

    How to Handle Large Changes to Your Data. 79

9. Calculated Fields and Items. **82**

    Example Data for Calculated Fields and Items. 82

    Adding A Calculated Field. 83

    Adding A Calculated Item. 86

Try Our Other Books **90**

1. What is a Pivot Table?

A pivot tool is a powerful and intuitive data analysis tool. that will help you get a far better understanding of your data. Especially if you have large amounts of data. Which of course leads to you making better business decisions.

By using a pivot table, you can quickly and easily summarise, analyze, explore and even present your data. And all it takes is just a few mouse clicks!

Pivot charts allow you to graphically and interactively explore your data. Just by clicking on "slicer" buttons you can redefine your data on the fly. Quickly and easily including and excluding data at will.

By following the examples in this book, you will be able to produce your first pivot table within an hour! It really is that easy.

Example Data for Our First Pivot Table.

For this exercise, we will use sales data from a fictitious furniture company called "Sofa, So Good" (see what I did there).

They are a growing company and have 6 stores dotted around the UK. They have 5 different product lines that they specialize in;

- Beds
- Single seater chairs
- Multiple seater chairs
- Storage
- Tables

The raw data for their sales can be found in the **Chapter 1** tab of the accompanying spreadsheet.

	A	B	C	D	E	F
1	Order Numb	Product	Category	Store	Date	Amount
2	1	Canopy bed	Beds	Manchester	2016/01/04	£185.94
3	2	Changing table	Tables	Birmingham	2016/01/06	£241.43
4	3	Canopy bed	Beds	Bristol	2016/01/17	£598.31
5	4	Davenport	Multiple Seat Chairs	London	2016/01/24	£310.59
6	5	Changing table	Tables	London	2016/01/26	£151.68
7	6	Bathroom cabinet	Storage	Manchester	2016/02/02	£76.85
8	7	Bunk bed	Beds	Cardiff	2016/02/03	£541.36
9	8	Chest of drawers	Storage	Birmingham	2016/02/08	£122.63
10	9	Bathroom cabinet	Storage	Manchester	2016/02/14	£116.86

Image 1-1 – Some of the annual sales data from "Sofa, So Good".

Without a lot of manual processing, the sales manager at "Sofa, So Good" has no idea of the value of the sales per product line, individual furniture model or even the sales per store.

This is where the power of pivot tables come in.

Step 1 – Creating Our Pivot Table.

Now we get to create our first pivot table! It is so easy it will only take a few mouse clicks

1. Click on any cell within your data. It does not matter which cell, as long as it inside your range of data.

2. Go to the **Insert** tab of the Excel ribbon and click on the Pivot Table option.

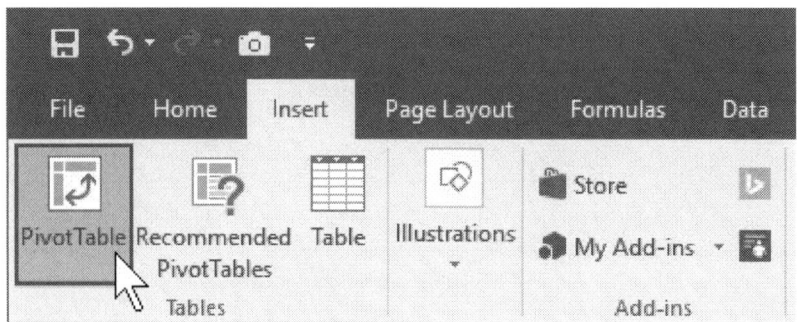

Image 1-2 – Selections to insert a pivot table.

That will bring up this pop up form;

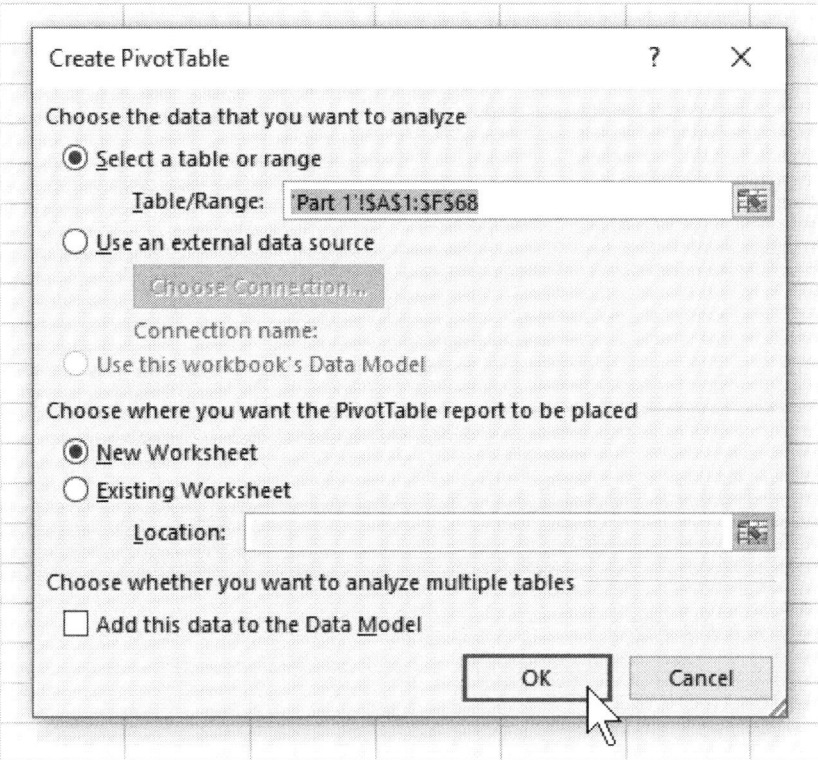

Image 1-3 – Create Pivot Table pop up form.

There are only two basic settings on this form.

- **"Choose the data that you want to analyze"** – This section of the form is used to identify where your raw data is stored. In this exercise, we will be using the **"Select a table or range"** option.

- **"Choose where you want your Pivot Table report to be placed"** – This is where you want your pivot table to appear. In this exercise, we will opt for putting it in a **"New Worksheet"**.

Excel should have automatically selected the data range for you. Based on the cell you had selected in the first step. Excel should have expanded your selection to the extremities of your data range. If it hasn't selected your range correctly, you can select the range manually in the usual fashion.

HANDY TIP - It is always good practice in Excel to keep data and reports separate. It is almost guaranteed that at some point in the future, either your report or your data layout will change. If your data and reports are mixed, this can be a minefield to unpick.

So, when it comes to choosing where you want your pivot table to appear, I would recommend leaving the **New Worksheet** option selected.

3. When you are happy with your selections click **OK**.

This will take you to your blank pivot table report and your screen will look like this;

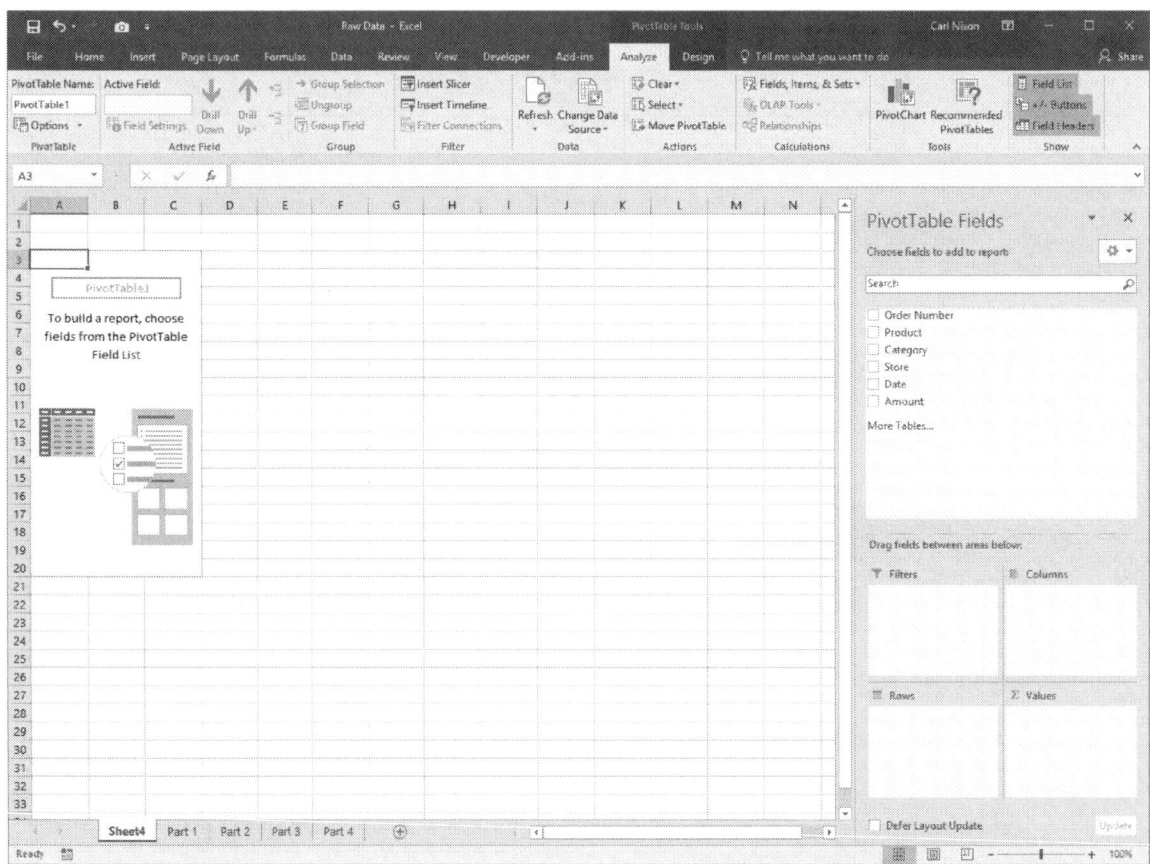

Image 1-4 – Our blank pivot table ready for populating.

To the left, we can see our blank and unpopulated pivot table. At the moment, it doesn't look very exciting, but that is just because it is not populated yet.

To the right of the spreadsheet is the pivot table Fields area. This is the area where you will define what your pivot table should do and how it should do it.

HANDY TIP - The Pivot Table Fields area is only visible when working on your pivot table. If you cannot see the Pivot Table Fields area, simply click on your pivot table and it will become visible again.

Step 2 – Populating Our Pivot Table.

We now have our blank pivot table, so let's start to populate it with our fields. In the Pivot Table Fields area make the following selections;

1. Select **Category**, **Store** and **Amount**.

2. Click on the Store field again and drag it down to the Filters area as show.

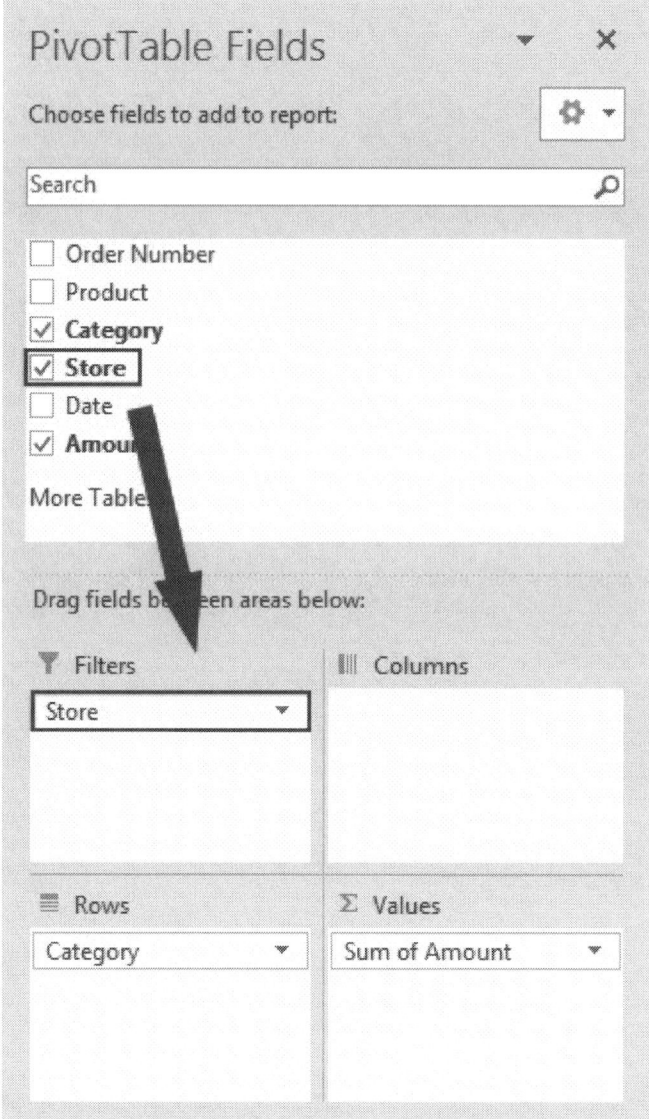

Image 1-5 – Our Pivot Table Fields selections.

If we look at our pivot table, we now have a fully functioning pivot table. It shows the breakdown of sales by category across the whole company.

A fully working pivot table in 7 mouse clicks!

	A	B
1	Store	(All)
2		
3	**Row Labels**	**Sum of Amount**
4	Beds	5139.33
5	Multiple Seat Chairs	1776.63
6	Single Seat Chairs	919.31
7	Storage	2054.68
8	Tables	3639.03
9	**Grand Total**	**13528.98**
10		

Image 1-6 – Our populated pivot table.

We can tell it is for the whole area by the **All** selection at the top.

To change the headings "Row Labels" and "Sum of Amount" to something more meaningful, do the following;

1. Click on the heading you want to change.

2. Press **F2**.

3. Type in the new headings.

As simple as that.

Step 3 – Using Our Pivot Table.

If we want to see the total sales for individual offices, we just change the All selection, at the top of our pivot table, to the office of our choice.

	A	B
1	Store	Bristol .T
2		
3	**Product Group** ▼	**Total Sales**
4	Beds	1119.09
5	Multiple Seat Chairs	512.8
6	Single Seat Chairs	306.92
7	Storage	61.93
8	Tables	444.16
9	Grand Total	2444.9
10		

Image 1-7 – Our pivot table for the Bristol store.

In this example, we are looking at the results for the Bristol store as indicated by the **Bristol** selection at the top of the pivot table. Note that the filtered icon appears to the right of the word Bristol to indicate that these are filtered results.

In the image below (Image 1-8), I have changed the column headings to something more meaningful (**Product Group** and **Total Sales**)

If we were only interested in a selection of product groups, chairs for example, we can further refine our pivot table.

1. Click the **Product Group** drop down arrow.

2. From the selections available, select **Multiple Seat Chairs** and **Single Seat Chairs**.

3. Click OK.

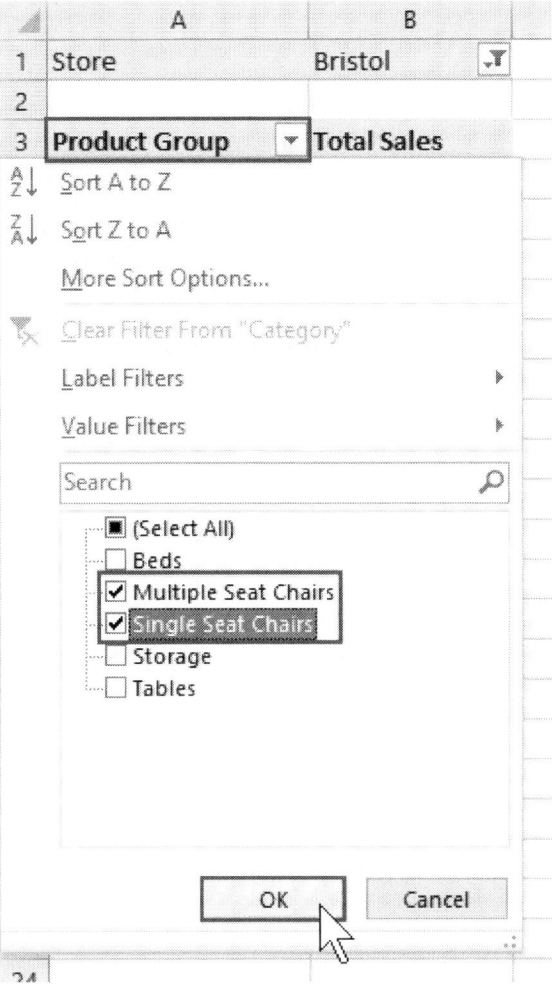

Image 1-8 – Refining our pivot table selections to show chairs only.

When we have made our selections, our pivot table will update to show this;

	A	B
1	Store	Bristol
2		
3	**Product Group**	**Total Sales**
4	Multiple Seat Chairs	512.8
5	Single Seat Chairs	306.92
6	**Grand Total**	**819.72**
7		

Image 1-9 – Our refined pivot table selections in action.

As a result of our choices, our pivot table is now only showing figures for the sales of chairs in the Bristol store.

That was a really simple example of how easy it is to interact with a pivot table. We will now start to add further levels of interaction and increase the overall usefulness of our pivot table.

Step 4 – Getting Even More Information from Our Pivot Table.

Automatically summing up data is a great time saver, but sometimes we need to extract other information such as the overall number of sales or average sales value. Pivot tables have you covered there as well.

If you haven't already done so, set your **Store** field to **All** and your **Product Group** field to **All**. Then follow these simple steps.

1. Select one of the **Total Sales** values in your **Pivot Table** (it doesn't matter which cell it is as long as it is in the **Total Sales** column).

2. Right click on the cell and select **Summarize Values By** from the menu that opens up.

3. Select if you want to see a **Count**, the **Average** value, the **Min**imum value or the **Max**imum value. In this example, we are selecting count.

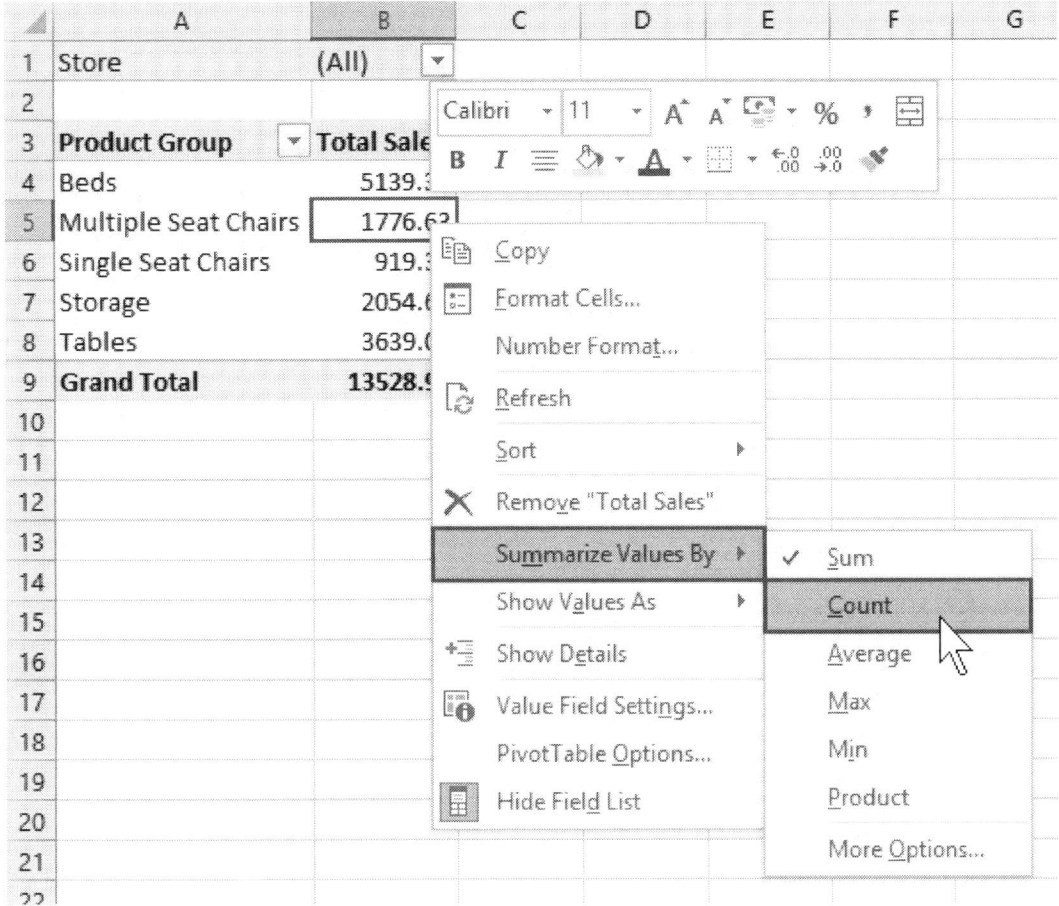

Image 1-10 – Opting to see sales counts rather than totals.

Once you have made your selections your pivot table will update as shown here;

	A	B
1	Store	(All)
2		
3	**Product Group**	Count of Amount
4	Beds	14
5	Multiple Seat Chairs	5
6	Single Seat Chairs	8
7	Storage	20
8	Tables	20
9	**Grand Total**	67

Image 1-11 – Our pivot table now shows sales counts rather than totals.

Step 5 – Adding Another Dimension to Our Pivot Table.

What if we wanted to see a table that shows a breakdown of the store, by sales of each product group? This would need a table with multiple columns.

In this exercise, we will set up a table with rows for product types and columns for stores. To do this we just rearrange our selections.

1. Drag **Store** out of **Filters** in to Columns.

2. Ensure **Category** is in **Rows**.

3. Ensure **Sum of Amount** is in **Values**.

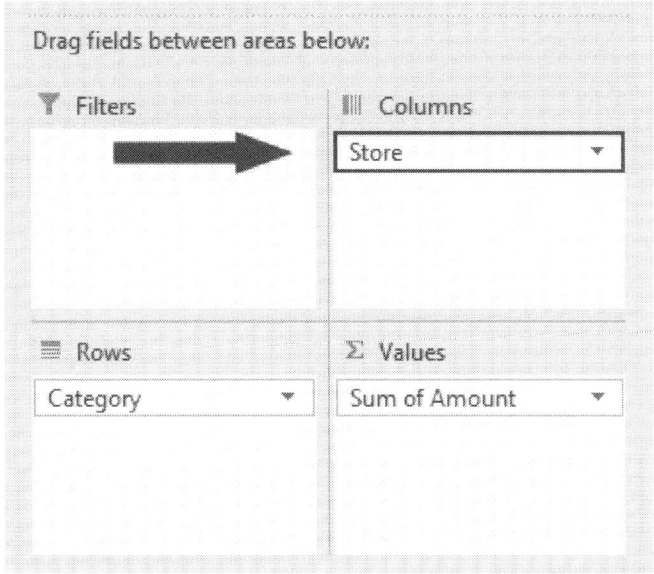

Image 1-12 — Creating a two-dimensional pivot table.

This will convert your pivot table in to this two-dimensional table like this;

Sum of Amount	Column Labels						
Product Group	Birmingham	Bristol	Cardiff	London	Manchester	Swindon	Grand Total
Beds	1194.68	1119.09	541.36	1247.57	899.94	136.69	5139.33
Multiple Seat Chairs		512.8	212.19	310.59	391.73	349.32	1776.63
Single Seat Chairs		306.92		387.57	90.02	134.8	919.31
Storage	661.66	61.93	374.7	202.6	349.99	403.8	2054.68
Tables	336.21	444.16	557.18	1539.69		761.79	3639.03
Grand Total	2192.55	2444.9	1685.43	3688.02	1731.68	1786.4	13528.98

Image 1-13 — Our two-dimensional pivot table.

If you drag the **Store** field from the **Columns** area to the **Rows** area, and then drag the **Category** field from the **Rows** area to the **Columns** area, your pivot table will have stores as rows and product types as columns.

Summary.

In this chapter, we have discovered pivot tables are far easier than they sound or look. We covered the basics of pivot tables and I'm sure it is already clear to you how simple and powerful they are. Experiment with the accompanying spreadsheet or some of your own data.

2. Grouping Pivot Table Items.

In **chapter 1** we looked at the sales data from an imaginary furniture shop called "Sofa, So Good". In the sales data we used in that exercise, we had different types of furniture grouped by type (beds, tables, storage etc.). However, in the real-world data doesn't always come neatly grouped up like that, so in this exercise we will look at adding grouping at the analysis / reporting stage.

Example Data for Grouping in Our Pivot Tables.

The raw data for this tutorial can found be in the **Chapter 2** tab of the accompanying spreadsheet.

Without the grouping column, the data looks like this;

	A	B	C	D	E
1	Order Numb	Product	Store	Date	Amount
2	1	Canopy bed	Manchester	2016/01/04	£185.94
3	2	Changing table	Birmingham	2016/01/06	£241.43
4	3	Canopy bed	Bristol	2016/01/17	£598.31
5	4	Davenport	London	2016/01/24	£310.59
6	5	Changing table	London	2016/01/26	£151.68
7	6	Bathroom cabinet	Manchester	2016/02/02	£76.85
8	7	Bunk bed	Cardiff	2016/02/03	£541.36
9	8	Chest of drawers	Birmingham	2016/02/08	£122.63
10	9	Bathroom cabinet	Manchester	2016/02/14	£116.86

Image 2-1 – The annual sales data from "Sofa, So Good" without any grouping data.

As you can see from the data, there is no easy way of finding sales figures per furniture type. So how do we find out the value of bed sales compared to chair sales?

Grouping Text Items in Pivot Tables.

These simple steps will allow you to group your data in to product types.

1. Use the data in the **Chapter 2** tab of the accompanying spreadsheet to create a pivot table using these settings;

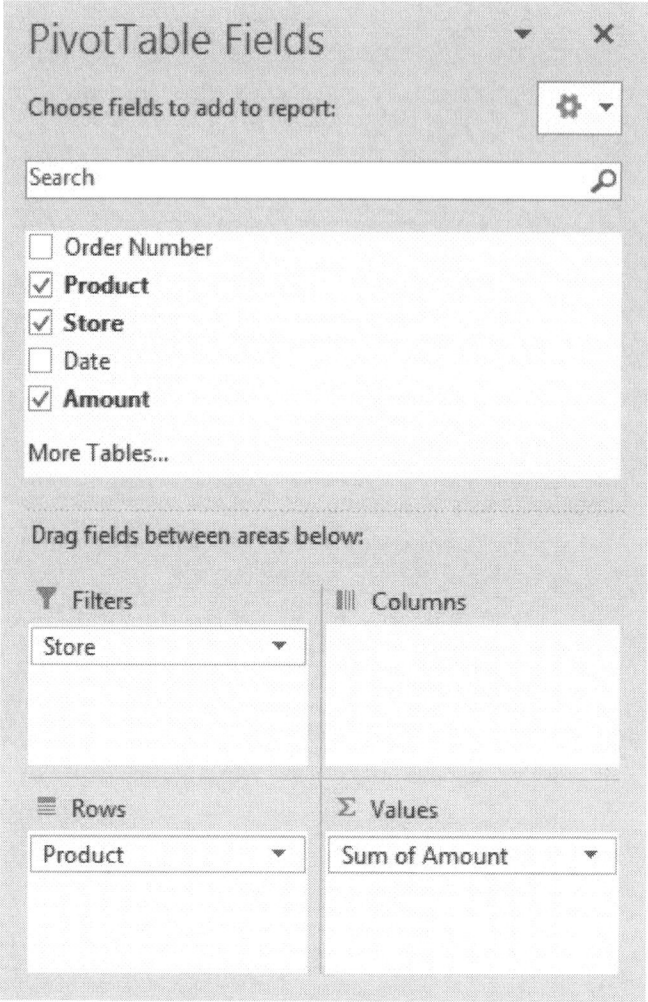

Image 2-2 – The initial selections for our pivot table.

2. Your pivot table should look like this;

	A	B
1	Store	(All)
2		
3	Row Labels	Sum of Amount
4	Bar Stool	198.1
5	Bathroom cabinet	355.34
6	Bean bag	268.13
7	Bed	1153.85
8	Bench	349.32
9	Bookcase	395.96
10	Bunk bed	1466.15
11	Canopy bed	1248.95
12	Chair	205.63
13	Chaise longue	144.78
14	Changing table	676.1
15	Chest	330.62
16	Chest of drawers	356.95
17	Coat rack	332.52
18	Coffee table	662.86

Image 2-3 – Our initial pivot table.

3. Select the items you want to group by holding down the Control key and clicking each item to be grouped in the pivot table.

4. Right click on one of the selected items and select **Group**. In **image 2-4**, we are grouping the bed products together.

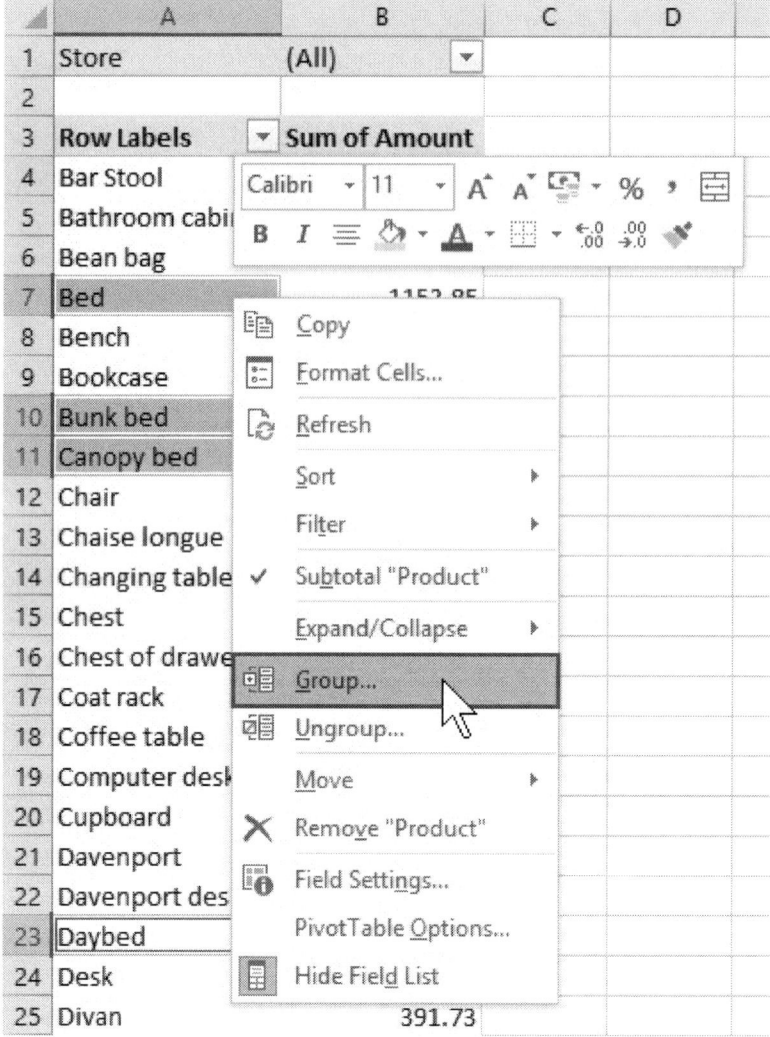

Image 2-4 – Grouping beds together.

When you click **Group** your table will look like this;

	A	B
1	Store	(All)
2		
3	Row Labels	Sum of Amount
4	⊟ Bar Stool	
5	Bar Stool	198.1
6	⊟ Bathroom cabinet	
7	Bathroom cabinet	355.34
8	⊟ Bean bag	
9	Bean bag	268.13
10	⊟ Group1	
11	Bed	1153.85
12	Bunk bed	1466.15
13	Canopy bed	1248.95
14	Daybed	871.6
15	Four-poster bed	398.78
16	⊟ Bench	
17	Bench	349.32
18	⊟ Bookcase	

Image 2-5 –Our new bed group.

Excel unimaginatively and automatically names our grouping as **Group 1**. This is not very user friendly, so we need to change that.

5. Click on the **Group 1** title.

6. Press **F2** and enter the new name as Beds.

7. Click the minus symbol to the left of our new title to collapse the group.

Repeat these steps for each of the groups until you get a pivot table that looks like this;

	A	B
1	Store	(All)
2		
3	Row Labels	Sum of Amount
4	⊞ Single Seat Chair	919.31
5	⊞ Storage	2054.68
6	⊞ Beds	5139.33
7	⊞ Multiple Seat Chairs	1776.63
8	⊞ Tables	3639.03
9	Grand Total	13528.98

Image 2-6 – Our grouped Pivot Table.

And that is it. Our items are now grouped in to handy categories without any categories being included in the original data its self.

Grouping Items in Pivot Tables by Dates.

A lot of reports need to be analyzed by dates or date ranges, and pivot tables offer us some powerful options to do this.

For this tutorial, we will need to create a new pivot table using the same data and the following settings.

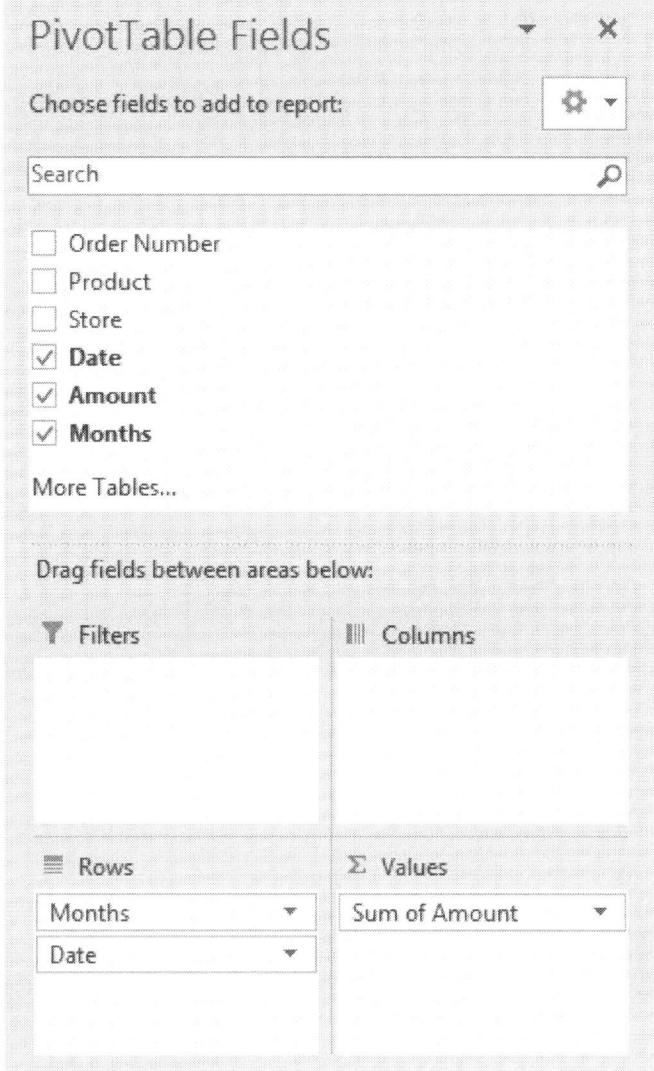

Image 2-7 –Selections for our fresh Pivot Table.

Note – When you select **Date** and **Amount**, Excel will automatically add the **Months** option for you.

This will produce a pivot table that looks like this;

	A	B
3	Row Labels	Sum of Amount
4	⊞ Jan	1487.95
5	⊞ Feb	1281.09
6	⊞ Mar	1668.93
7	⊞ Apr	1473.21
8	⊞ May	108.08
9	⊞ Jun	968.35
10	⊞ Jul	466.52
11	⊞ Aug	1652.97
12	⊞ Sep	1104.82
13	⊞ Oct	2322.85
14	⊞ Nov	700.15
15	⊞ Dec	294.06
16	Grand Total	13528.98

Image 2-8 – Excel automatically groups dates by months.

The automatic grouping by months is really handy in a lot of situations, but what if we want to report by week or quarter?

The first step is to get rid of the month groupings that Excel applied. We do this by unticking the **Months** option in the **Pivot Table Fields** area.

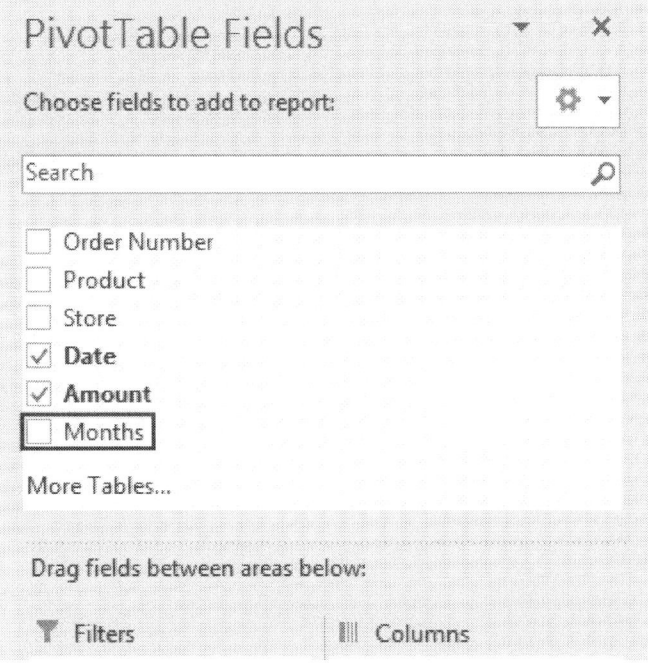

Image 2-9 –Untick the Months selection.

This will remove the grouping by Month and show data by individual dates like this;

	A	B
3	Row Labels	Sum of Amount
4	04-Jan	185.94
5	06-Jan	241.43
6	17-Jan	598.31
7	24-Jan	310.59
8	26-Jan	151.68
9	02-Feb	76.85
10	03-Feb	541.36
11	08-Feb	122.63
12	14-Feb	116.86
13	17-Feb	139.3
14	21-Feb	284.09
15	01-Mar	125.22
16	04-Mar	370.81
17	05-Mar	136.82
18	06-Mar	541.32

Image 2-10 –Date based pivot table without grouping by Month.

Right click on one of the dates and select **Group**.

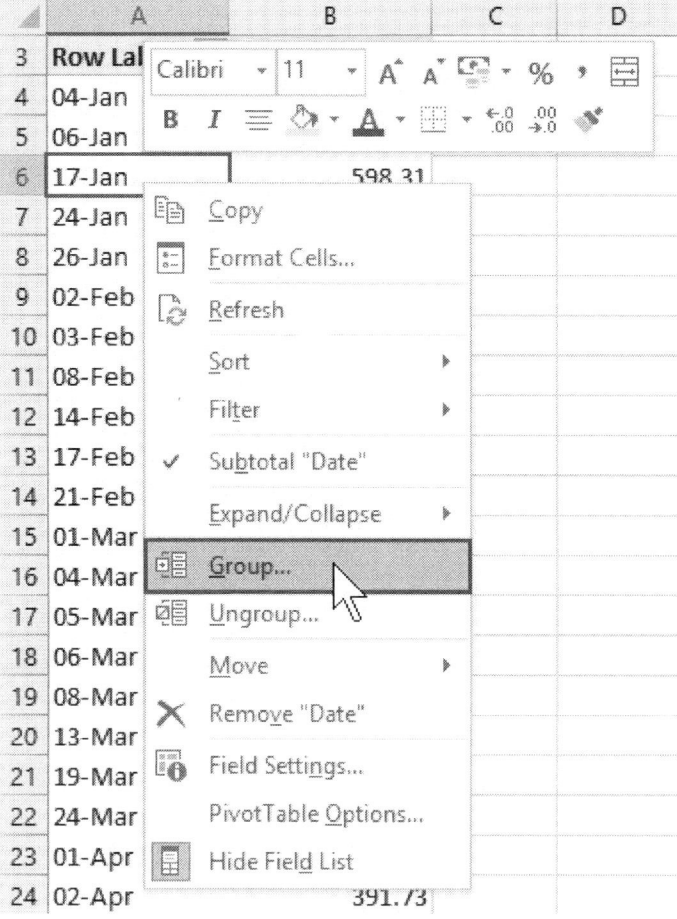

Image 2-11 –Grouping by dates.

When you click **Group**, Excel will automatically detect you are trying to group by date and display this pop up form.

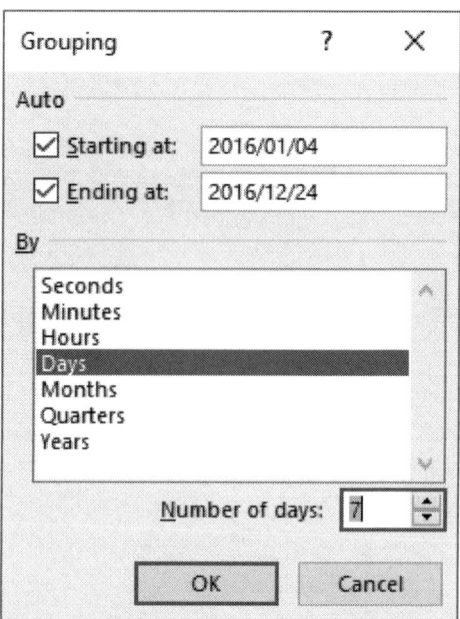

Image 2-12–Pivot Table broken down by week.
US Readers Note – *The dates in the above image are in the UK date format of dd/mm/yyyy.*

If you want to change the first date or last date of the weekly breakdowns, set them in the **Starting at** and **Ending at** fields.

	A	B
3	Row Labels	Sum of Amount
4	2016/01/04 - 2016/01/10	427.37
5	2016/01/11 - 2016/01/17	598.31
6	2016/01/18 - 2016/01/24	310.59
7	2016/01/25 - 2016/01/31	151.68
8	2016/02/01 - 2016/02/07	618.21
9	2016/02/08 - 2016/02/14	239.49
10	2016/02/15 - 2016/02/21	423.39
11	2016/02/29 - 2016/03/06	1174.17
12	2016/03/07 - 2016/03/13	279.06

Image 2-13 – Changing our selections to Months and Quarters.
US Readers Note – *The dates in the above image are in the UK date format of dd/mm/yyyy.*

If you right click on one of the dates and select **Group** again we will end up back at the pop up form. This time unselect **Days** and select **Months** and **Quarters**.

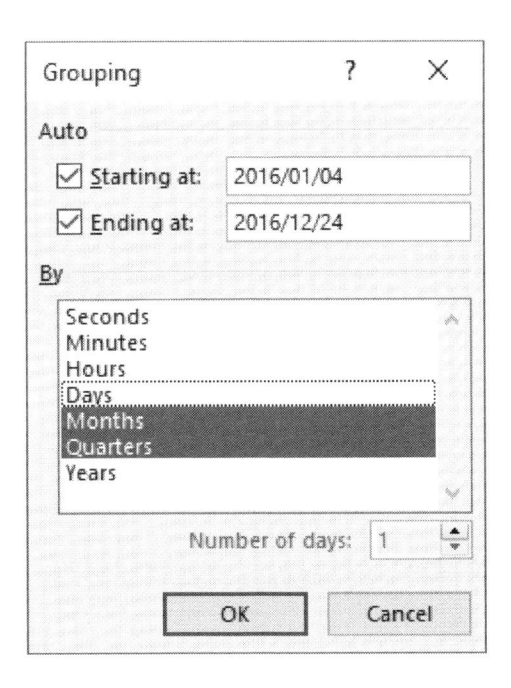

Image 2-14 – Changing our selections to Months and Quarters.
US Readers Note – *The dates in the above image are in the UK date format of dd/mm/yyyy.*

This will give us a handy month by month and quarter breakdown of the figures.

	A	B
3	Row Labels	Sum of Amount
4	⊞ Qtr1	4437.97
5	⊟ Qtr2	
6	Apr	1473.21
7	May	108.08
8	Jun	968.35
9	⊞ Qtr3	3224.31
10	⊞ Qtr4	3317.06
11	Grand Total	13528.98

Image 2-15 –Pivot table broken down by months and quarters.

Summary.

And there we have it, in a few short steps we have grouped up our results in to more meaningful figures. This ability is really handy when there is no grouping available in the raw data.

3. Same Pivot Table, Different Look.

As you browse the internet looking for a help on pivot tables, you will find 2 different styles of pivot tables. This can be confusing when looking for help, so we will cover the differences here.

The differences are purely cosmetic and both styles of pivot tables do exactly the same thing. Which of the two styles you should use comes down to your own personal tastes and preferences.

Example Data for Our Pivot Table.

The raw data for this exercise can be found in the **Chapter 3** tab of the accompanying spreadsheet.

This is what our data looks like;

	A	B	C	D	E	F
1	Order Numb	Product	Category	Store	Date	Amount
2	1	Canopy bed	Beds	Manchester	2016/01/04	£185.94
3	2	Changing table	Tables	Birmingham	2016/01/06	£241.43
4	3	Canopy bed	Beds	Bristol	2016/01/17	£598.31
5	4	Davenport	Multiple Seat Chairs	London	2016/01/24	£310.59
6	5	Changing table	Tables	London	2016/01/26	£151.68
7	6	Bathroom cabinet	Storage	Manchester	2016/02/02	£76.85
8	7	Bunk bed	Beds	Cardiff	2016/02/03	£541.36
9	8	Chest of drawers	Storage	Birmingham	2016/02/08	£122.63
10	9	Bathroom cabinet	Storage	Manchester	2016/02/14	£116.86
11	10	Coat rack	Storage	Swindon	2016/02/17	£139.30
12	12	Daybed	Beds	Manchester	2016/02/21	£149.29

Image 3-1 – The annual sales data from "Sofa, So Good".

Setting Up a Pivot Table.

First, create a pivot table as detailed in **chapter 1**. Use the following selections in the Pivot Fields Area;

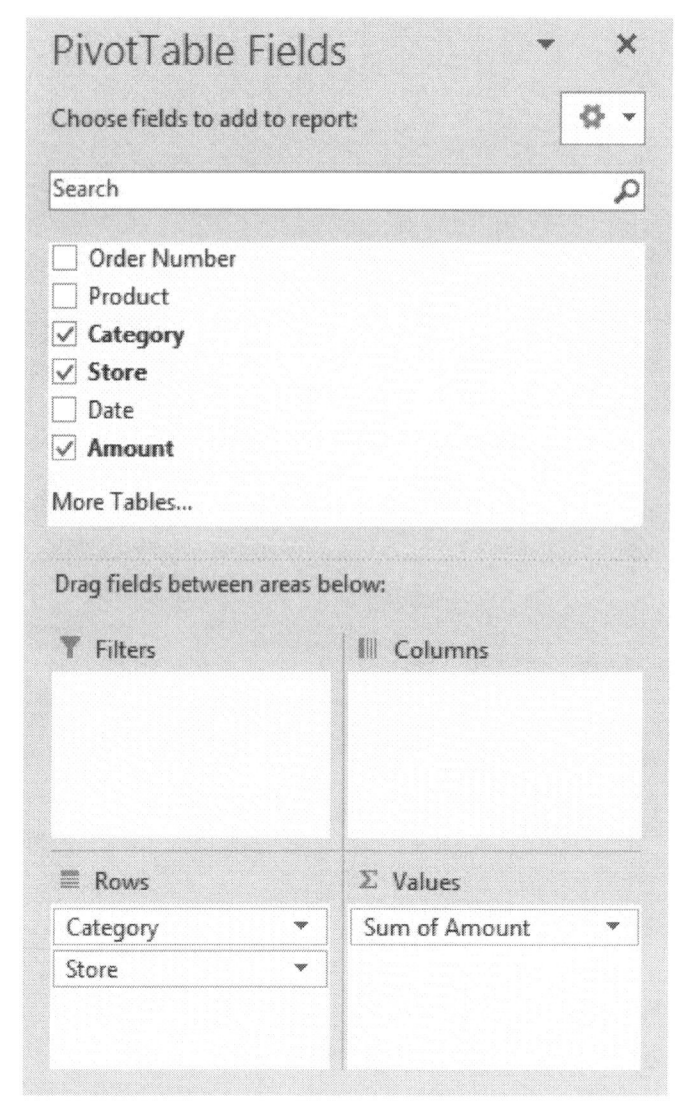

Image 3-2 – Our selections for our pivot table.

This will create a pivot table that looks like this;

	A	B
3	Row Labels	Sum of Amount
4	⊟ Beds	5139.33
5	Birmingham	1194.68
6	Bristol	1119.09
7	Cardiff	541.36
8	London	1247.57
9	Manchester	899.94
10	Swindon	136.69
11	⊟ Multiple Seat Chairs	1776.63
12	Bristol	512.8
13	Cardiff	212.19
14	London	310.59
15	Manchester	391.73
16	Swindon	349.32
17	⊟ Single Seat Chairs	919.31
18	Bristol	306.92
19	London	387.57
20	Manchester	90.02
21	Swindon	134.8

Image 3-3 – Our pivot table.

There is no official name for this style of layout, so I will just refer to it as the "modern" style.

Right click any of the cells in the Pivot Table and select **Pivot Table Options...**

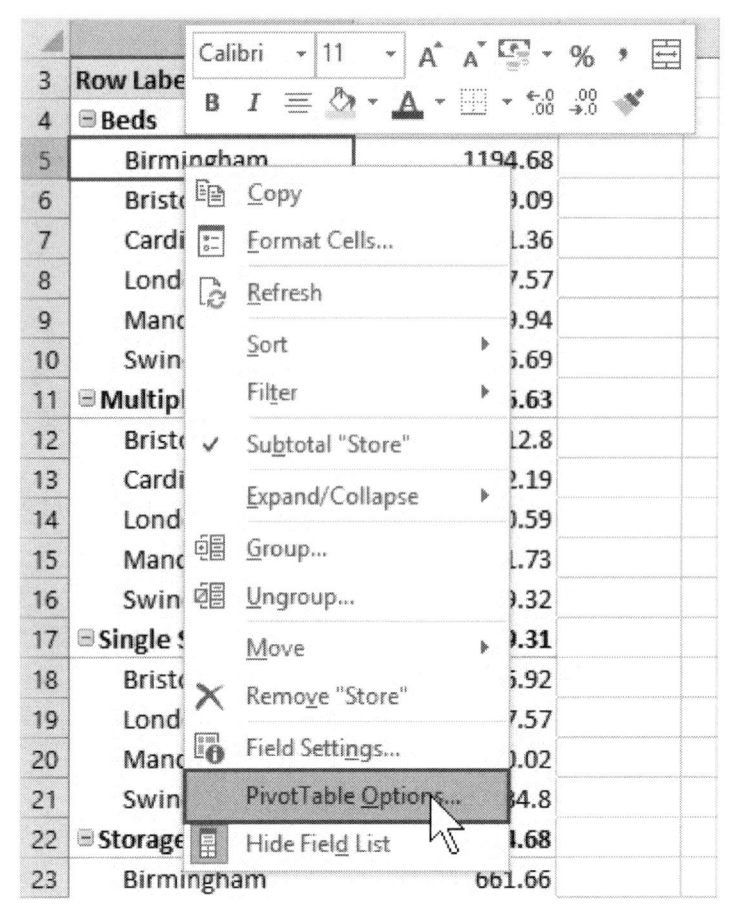

Image 3-4 – Selecting "PivotTable Options...".

This will bring up this form.

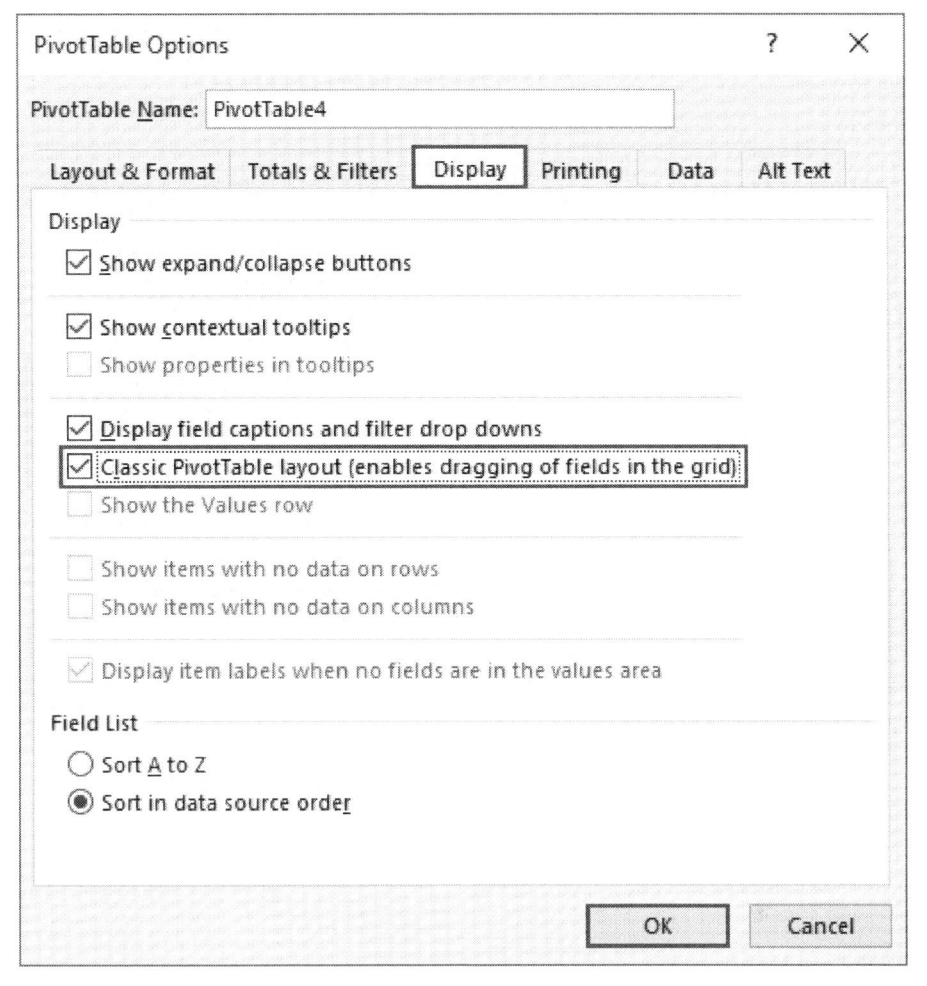

Image 3-5 – PivotTables Options Form.

When the form opens up, follow these steps;

1. Go to the **Display Tab**.

2. Tick the **Classic Pivot Table layout** option.

3. Click **OK**.

Now our pivot table looks like this;

	A	B	C
3	Sum of Amount		
4	Category	Store	Total
5	⊟ Beds	Birmingham	1194.68
6		Bristol	1119.09
7		Cardiff	541.36
8		London	1247.57
9		Manchester	899.94
10		Swindon	136.69
11	**Beds Total**		5139.33
12	⊟ **Multiple Seat Chairs**	Bristol	512.8
13		Cardiff	212.19
14		London	310.59
15		Manchester	391.73
16		Swindon	349.32
17	**Multiple Seat Chairs Total**		1776.63

Image 3-6 – A pivot table in the "Classic" layout.

This is the same pivot table as in **image 3-3** and none of the contents have changed. Just the look has changed.

There are some minor advantages to the "Classic" layout, but the choice between "Classic" and "Modern" is mostly an aesthetics choice.

4. Multi-Level Pivot Tables.

We are now going to the next level with our pivot tables and we will now introduce multiple row fields, multiple value fields and multiple report filter fields.

Example Data to be Multi-Levelled.

The raw data for this tutorial can found be in the **Chapter 4** tab of the accompanying spreadsheet.

This is what the data looks like;

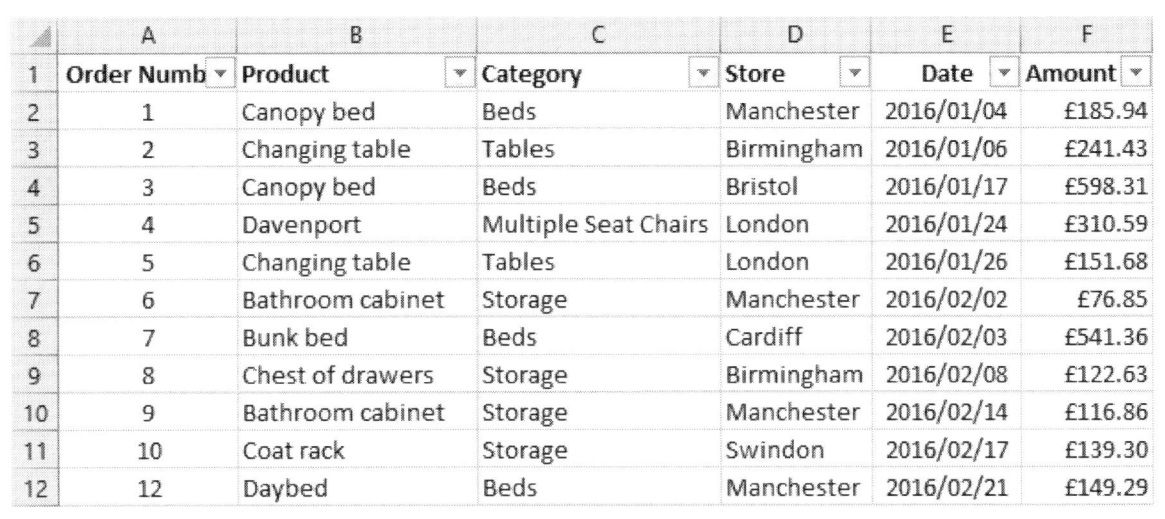

	A	B	C	D	E	F
1	Order Numb	Product	Category	Store	Date	Amount
2	1	Canopy bed	Beds	Manchester	2016/01/04	£185.94
3	2	Changing table	Tables	Birmingham	2016/01/06	£241.43
4	3	Canopy bed	Beds	Bristol	2016/01/17	£598.31
5	4	Davenport	Multiple Seat Chairs	London	2016/01/24	£310.59
6	5	Changing table	Tables	London	2016/01/26	£151.68
7	6	Bathroom cabinet	Storage	Manchester	2016/02/02	£76.85
8	7	Bunk bed	Beds	Cardiff	2016/02/03	£541.36
9	8	Chest of drawers	Storage	Birmingham	2016/02/08	£122.63
10	9	Bathroom cabinet	Storage	Manchester	2016/02/14	£116.86
11	10	Coat rack	Storage	Swindon	2016/02/17	£139.30
12	12	Daybed	Beds	Manchester	2016/02/21	£149.29

Image 4-1 – The annual sales data from "Sofa, So Good".

Using Multiple Row Fields.

First, create a pivot table as detailed in **chapter 1**. Use the following selections in the **Pivot Table Fields** Area;

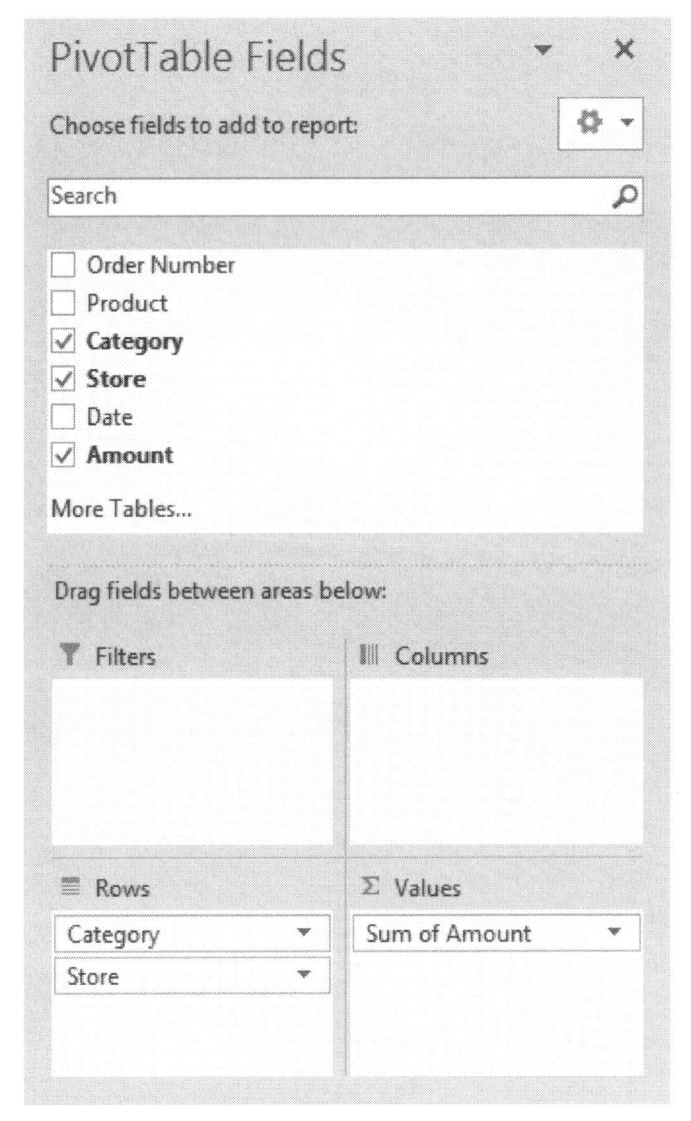

Image 4-2 – Our selections for our pivot table.

Our resultant pivot table looks like this (note it is in the "Classic" layout – see **chapter 3** for more details).

	A	B	C
3	Sum of Amount		
4	Category	Store	Total
5	⊟Beds	Birmingham	1194.68
6		Bristol	1119.09
7		Cardiff	541.36
8		London	1247.57
9		Manchester	899.94
10		Swindon	136.69
11	Beds Total		5139.33
12	⊟Multiple Seat Chairs	Bristol	512.8
13		Cardiff	212.19
14		London	310.59
15		Manchester	391.73
16		Swindon	349.32
17	Multiple Seat Chairs Total		1776.63
18	⊟Single Seat Chairs	Bristol	306.92
19		London	387.57
20		Manchester	90.02
21		Swindon	134.8
22	Single Seat Chairs Total		919.31

Image 4-3 – The resultant pivot table in the "Classic" layout.

Using Multiple Values.

We can expand our pivot table to show multiple values per field type. For example, we can show the total and the percentage of the overall total.

Create a new pivot table (using the same data) and use the following settings;

1. Tick **Store** and ensure it appears under rows.

2. Tick **Amount** and ensure it appears under values.

3. Click on and drag **Amount** down to Values.

In **Values**, you should have **Sum of Amount** and **Sum of Amount2** listed.

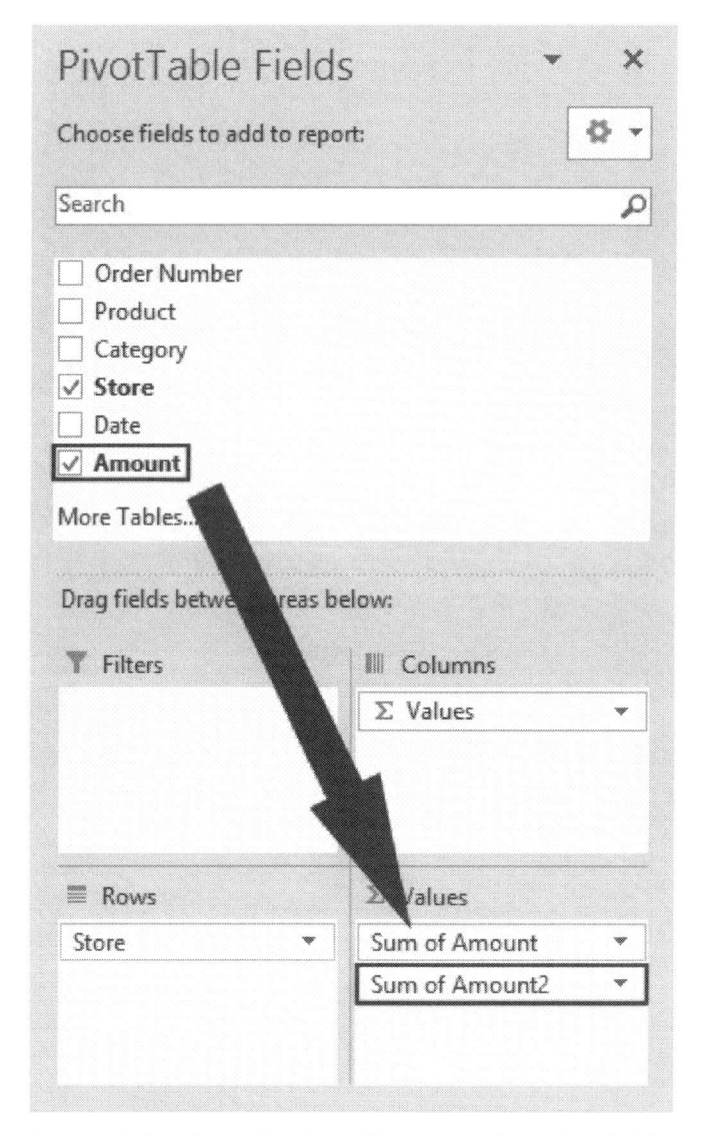

Image 4-4 – Our selections for our multi-value fields.

Once you have made these selections your pivot table will look like this;

	A	B	C
3		Values	
4	Store	Sum of Amount	Sum of Amount2
5	Birmingham	2192.55	2192.55
6	Bristol	2444.9	2444.9
7	Cardiff	1685.43	1685.43
8	London	3688.02	3688.02
9	Manchester	1731.68	1731.68
10	Swindon	1786.4	1786.4
11	Grand Total	13528.98	13528.98

Image 4-5 – Our resultant pivot table.

Obviously having two sets of totals that are the same is completely useless, so what can we do with this new element. Let's use the new column to show us what percentage of the grand total each subtotal represents.

Right click on any cell in the **Sum of Amount2** column and select **Value Field Settings**.

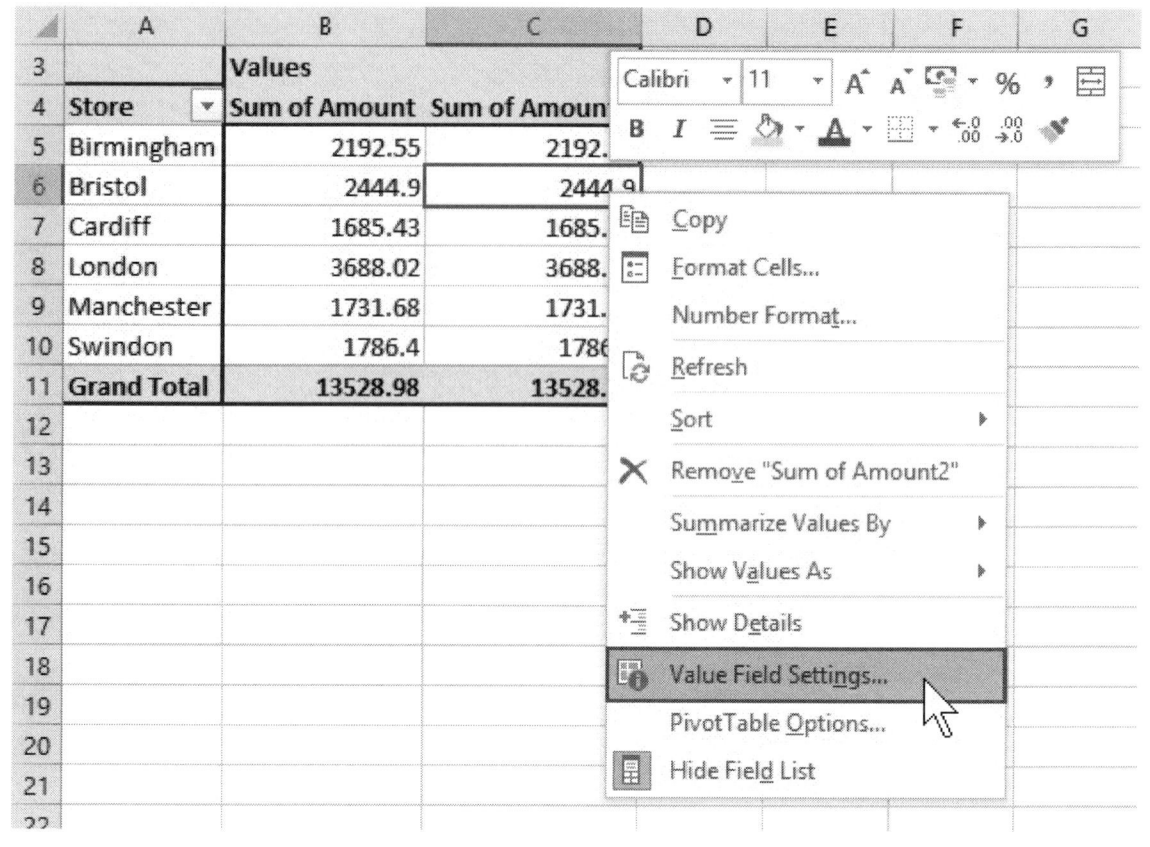

Image 4-6 – Locating and selecting "Value Field Settings...".

This will bring up the following form;

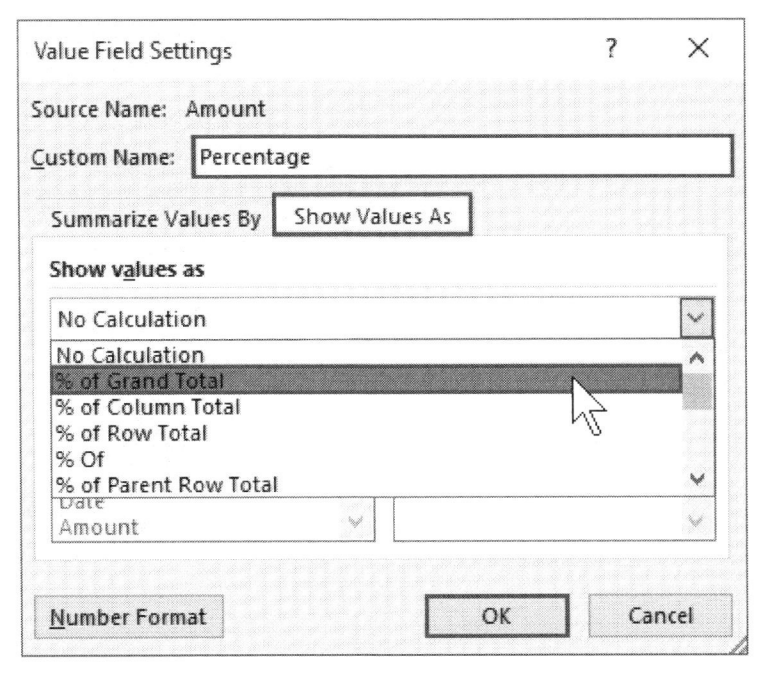

Image 4-7 – The Value Field Settings form.

Select the following options.

1. Set the Custom Name to **Percentage**.

2. Select the **Show Values** As tab.

3. Select **% of Grand Total** from the **Show values as** dropdown.

4. Click **OK**.

	A	B	C
3		Values	
4	Store	Sum of Amount	Percentage
5	Birmingham	2192.55	16.21%
6	Bristol	2444.9	18.07%
7	Cardiff	1685.43	12.46%
8	London	3688.02	27.26%
9	Manchester	1731.68	12.80%
10	Swindon	1786.4	13.20%
11	Grand Total	13528.98	100.00%

Image 4-8 – Our new pivot table with percentages.

We can now see what percentage of the sales each store contributes to the company's overall sales.

Multiple Report Filter Fields.

So, what if we want to search for specific orders that contain specific products sold in specific stores. For example, what it we wanted to find all the orders for coffee tables in the London store.

Create a new pivot table from the same data as before and use these settings.

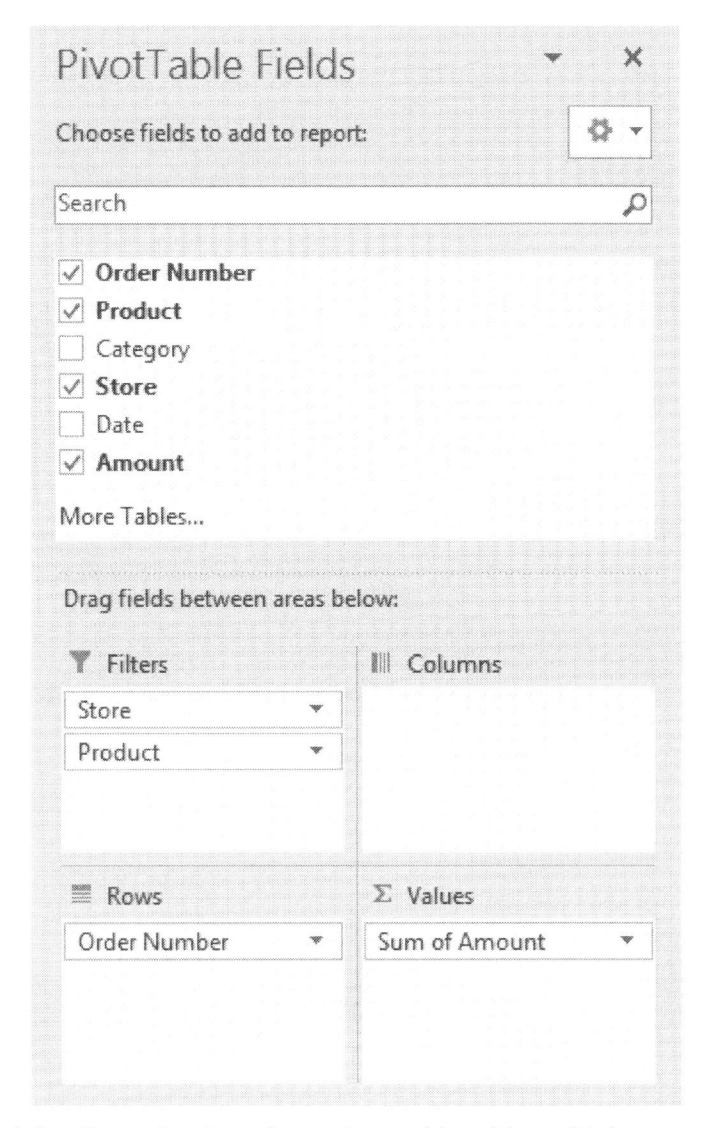

Image 4-9 – Our selections for a pivot table with multiple report filters.

1. Select **Order Number**, **Product**, **Store** and **Amount**.

2. Ensure **Store** and **Product** is in the **Filters** section.

3. Ensure **Order Number** is in the **Rows** section. **Note** – just selecting **Order Number** will not work, you will need to click on and drag **Order Number** from the top field selection area to the **Rows** section.

4. Ensure **Sum of Amount** is in the **Values** section.

Our pivot table now lists order numbers and their values, and should now look like this;

	A	B
1	Store	(All)
2	Product	(All)
3		
4	Row Labels	Sum of Amount
5	1	185.94
6	2	241.43
7	3	598.31
8	4	310.59
9	5	151.68
10	6	76.85
11	7	541.36
12	8	122.63
13	9	116.86
14	10	139.3
15	11	134.8
16	12	149.29

Image 4-10 – Our pivot table with multiple report filters.

We can now use the Store and Product filters to select **London** and **Coffee Table**. In our example data that identifies two orders.

	A	B
1	Store	London
2	Product	Coffee table
3		
4	Row Labels	Sum of Amount
5	14	270.78
6	45	163.95
7	Grand Total	434.73

Image 4-11 – Our pivot table with multiple filters to show sales of Coffee Tables from the London store.

Experiment with the filters to see what other information you can extract from the data.

5. Frequency Distribution in Pivot Tables.

Pivot tables can also be used to quickly produce frequency distribution figures from our data.

Example Data for a Frequency Distribution Pivot Table.

A copy of this data for this exercise can be found in the **Chapter 5** tab of the accompanying spreadsheet.

This is what our data looks like;

Order Number	Product	Category	Store	Date	Amount
1	Canopy bed	Beds	Manchester	2016/01/04	£185.94
2	Changing table	Tables	Birmingham	2016/01/06	£241.43
3	Canopy bed	Beds	Bristol	2016/01/17	£598.31
4	Davenport	Multiple Seat Chairs	London	2016/01/24	£310.59
5	Changing table	Tables	London	2016/01/26	£151.68
6	Bathroom cabinet	Storage	Manchester	2016/02/02	£76.85
7	Bunk bed	Beds	Cardiff	2016/02/03	£541.36
8	Chest of drawers	Storage	Birmingham	2016/02/08	£122.63
9	Bathroom cabinet	Storage	Manchester	2016/02/14	£116.86
10	Coat rack	Storage	Swindon	2016/02/17	£139.30
12	Daybed	Beds	Manchester	2016/02/21	£149.29

Image 5-1 – The annual sales data from "Sofa, So Good".

Finding Frequency Distribution Using Pivot Tables.

First, create a pivot table as detailed in **chapter 1** and use the following selections in the **PivotTable Fields** area.

Note - you will need to tick the **Amount** field and then click on and drag the **Amount** field down to the **Rows** section.

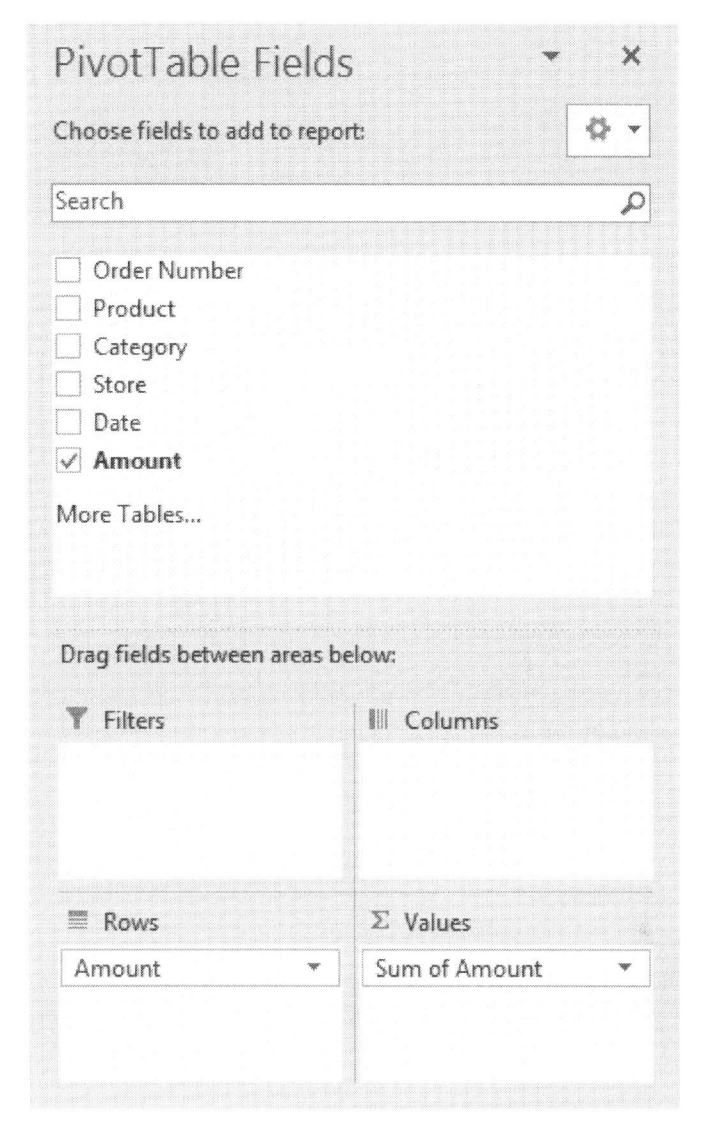

Image 5-2 – Our selections for our pivot table.

Our resultant pivot table looks like this;

	A	B
3	Row Labels	Sum of Amount
4	£61.93	61.93
5	£64.11	64.11
6	£67.35	67.35
7	£70.92	70.92
8	£76.58	76.58
9	£76.85	76.85
10	£77.38	77.38
11	£79.70	79.7
12	£90.02	90.02
13	£94.78	94.78
14	£99.70	99.7
15	£100.03	100.03
16	£102.67	102.67
17	£107.62	107.62
18	£108.08	108.08
19	£108.87	108.87

Image 5-3 – The resultant pivot table.

To group our values right click on any cell in the left column and select **Group...**

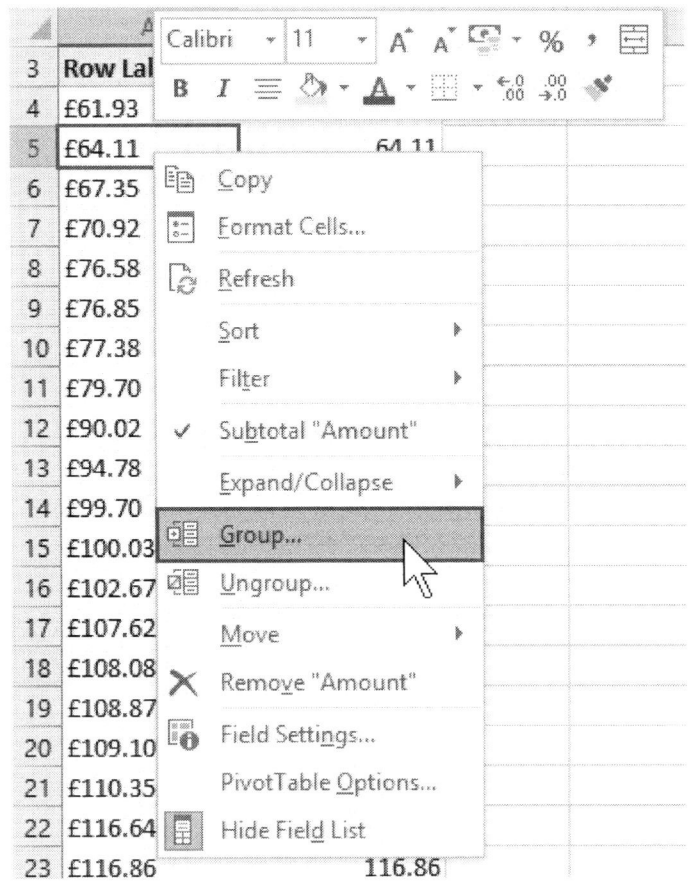

Image 5-4 – Grouping our results.

This will bring up the following window;

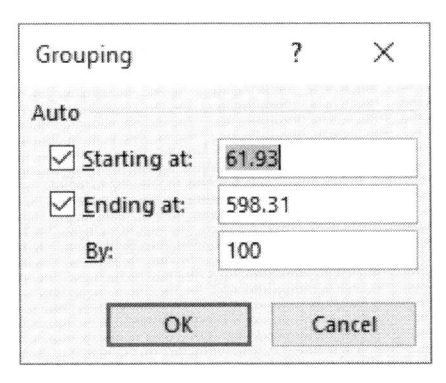

Image 5-5 – Our grouping options.

These options will result in the invoices being grouped into values of

£61.93 to £161.93

£161.93 to £261.93

...

£461.93 to £561.93

£561.93 to £661.93

Which is not very user friendly or meaningful. To group our invoices in £50 bands starting at £0 and ending at £600, change the settings to;

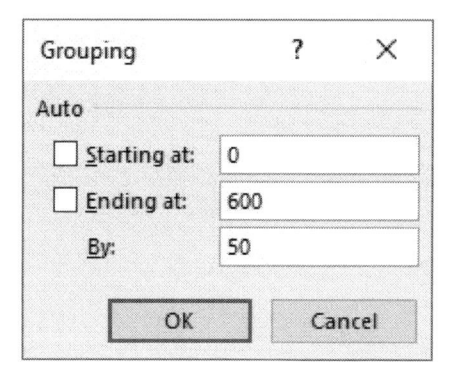

Image 5-6 – Our revised grouping options.

The resulting pivot table shows us the total sales in each group.

	A	B
3	Row Labels	Sum of Amount
4	50-100	859.32
5	100-150	3274.62
6	150-200	1359.48
7	200-250	1164.49
8	250-300	1082.3
9	300-350	962.15
10	350-400	775.45
11	400-450	404.01
12	450-500	932.59
13	500-550	2116.26
14	550-600	598.31
15	Grand Total	13528.98

Image 5-7 – Our grouped sales.

But what if we want to know how many sales were made in each band?

Right click on the right column then select **Summarize Values By** and then select **Count**.

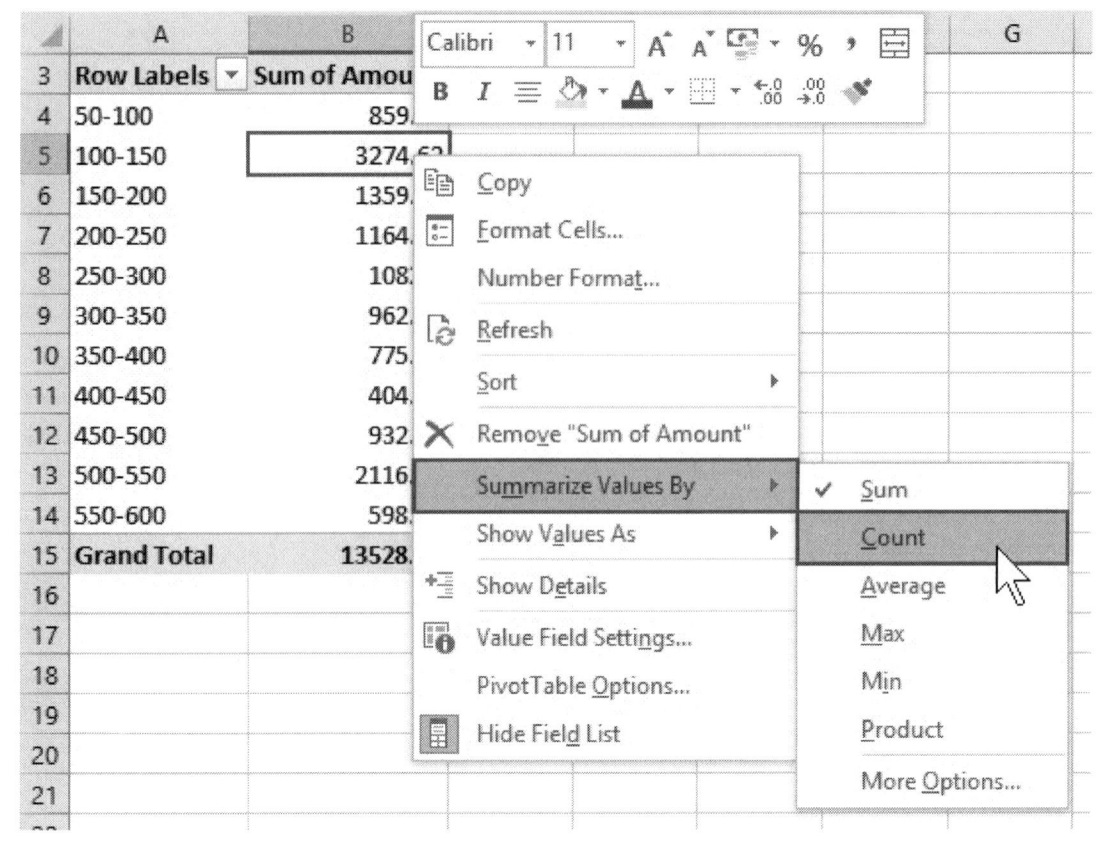

Image 5-8 – Changing our groups to counts rather than sums.

This updates our pivot table to show invoice counts.

	A	B
3	Row Labels	Count of Amount
4	50-100	11
5	100-150	26
6	150-200	8
7	200-250	5
8	250-300	4
9	300-350	3
10	350-400	2
11	400-450	1
12	450-500	2
13	500-550	4
14	550-600	1
15	**Grand Total**	67

Image 5-9 – Our groups now show invoice counts.

6. Charting with Pivot Charts.

From our pivot tables, we can quickly build some dynamic charts and graphs.

Example Data for Our Pivot Chart.

A copy of this data for this exercise can be found in the Chapter 6 – Data tab of the accompanying spreadsheet.

This is what our data looks like;

	A	B	C	D	E	F
1	Order Numb	Product	Category	Store	Date	Amount
2	1	Canopy bed	Beds	Manchester	2016/01/04	£185.94
3	2	Changing table	Tables	Birmingham	2016/01/06	£241.43
4	3	Canopy bed	Beds	Bristol	2016/01/17	£598.31
5	4	Davenport	Multiple Seat Chairs	London	2016/01/24	£310.59
6	5	Changing table	Tables	London	2016/01/26	£151.68
7	6	Bathroom cabinet	Storage	Manchester	2016/02/02	£76.85
8	7	Bunk bed	Beds	Cardiff	2016/02/03	£541.36
9	8	Chest of drawers	Storage	Birmingham	2016/02/08	£122.63
10	9	Bathroom cabinet	Storage	Manchester	2016/02/14	£116.86
11	10	Coat rack	Storage	Swindon	2016/02/17	£139.30
12	12	Daybed	Beds	Manchester	2016/02/21	£149.29

Image 6-1 – The annual sales data from "Sofa, So Good".

And from this data we will produce the two-dimensional pivot table found in the **Chapter 6 – Pivot Table** tab of the accompanying spreadsheet. Refer to **chapter 4** of this tutorial for details on how to build your own two-dimensional pivot table.

Sum of Amount	Column Labels					
Row Labels	Beds	Multiple Seat Chairs	Single Seat Chairs	Storage	Tables	Grand Total
Birmingham	1194.68			661.66	336.21	2192.55
Bristol	1119.09	512.8	306.92	61.93	444.16	2444.9
Cardiff	541.36	212.19		374.7	557.18	1685.43
London	1247.57	310.59	387.57	202.6	1539.69	3688.02
Manchester	899.94	391.73	90.02	349.99		1731.68
Swindon	136.69	349.32	134.8	403.8	761.79	1786.4
Grand Total	5139.33	1776.63	919.31	2054.68	3639.03	13528.98

Image 6-2 – Our two-dimensional pivot table.

Creating A Pivot Chart.

Follow these steps to produce our pivot chart;

1. Select any cell in the pivot table.

2. From the **Insert** menu select the style of chart you want. In the example below we have selected a 2D Column chart. If you are using an older version of Excel your chart selection process will be slightly different.

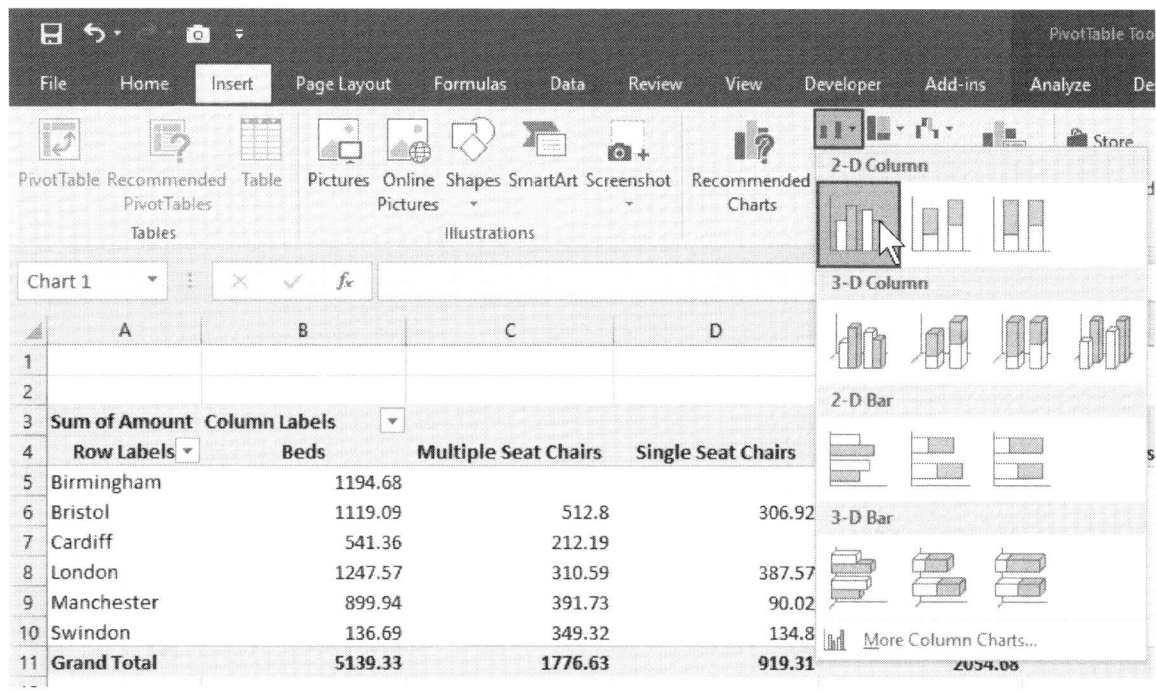

Image 6-3 – Selecting our style of chart.

This will result in a chart that looks like this;

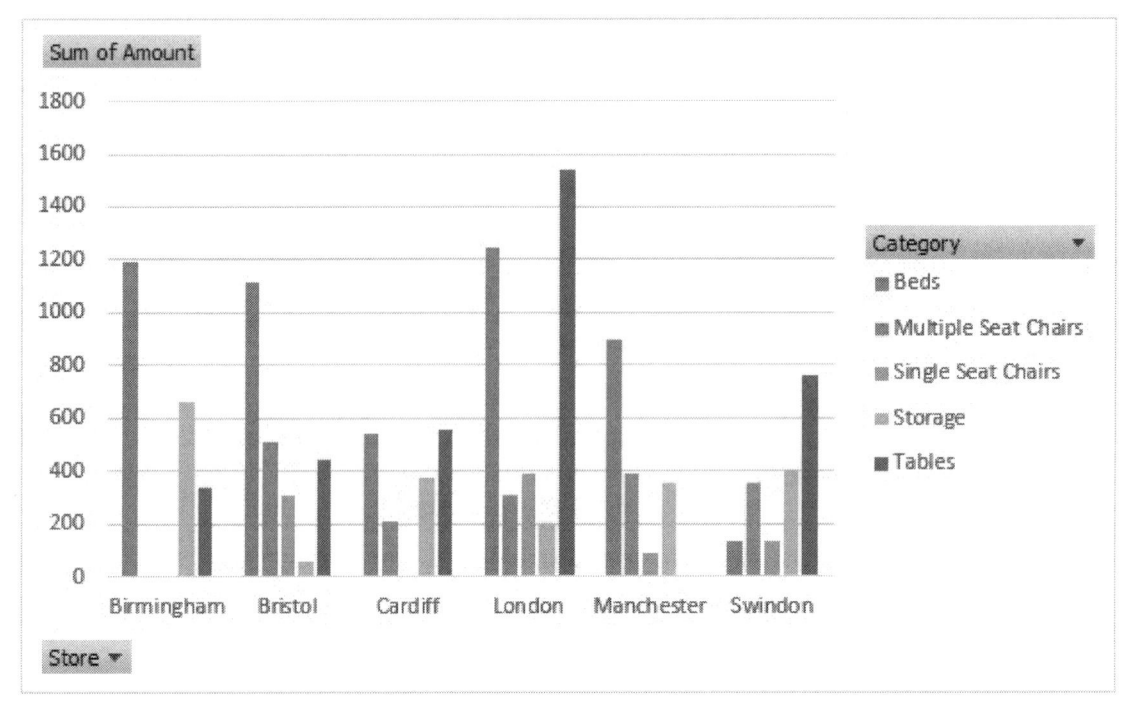

Image 6-4 – Our pivot chart.

Filtering Our Pivot Chart.

If we want to filter our results to show just the values for Cardiff and London (for example), we can do that directly in the chart.

1. Click on the **Store** filter button (bottom left corner).

2. Select **Cardiff** and **London** from the options available.

3. Click **OK**.

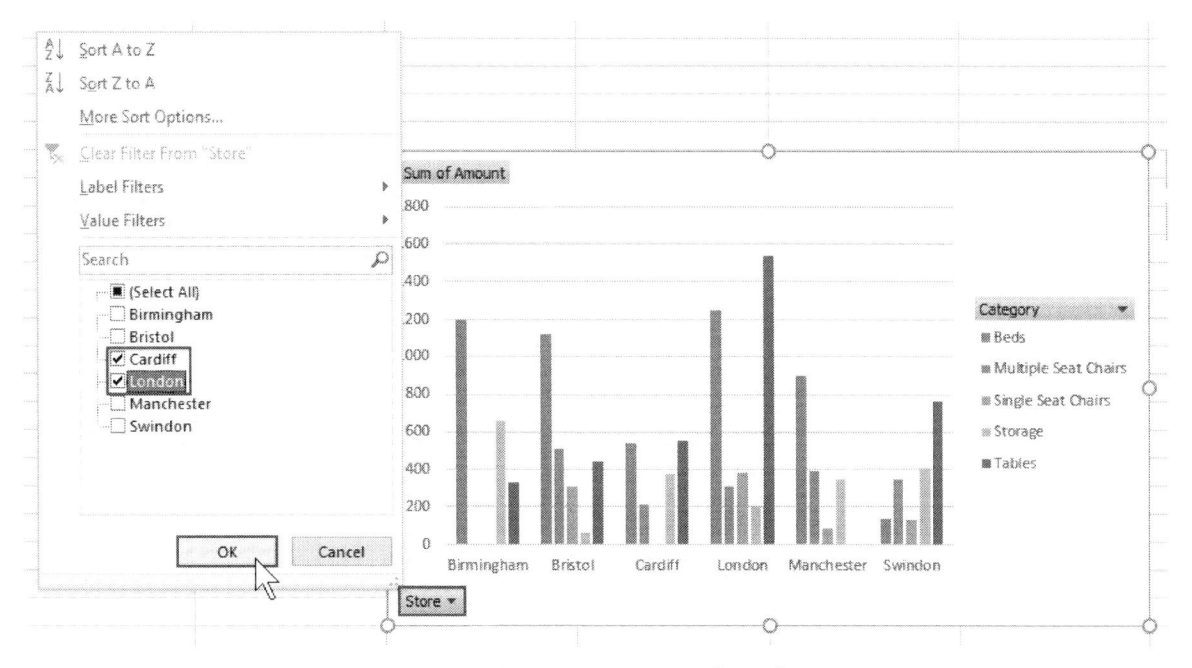

Image 6-5 – Filtering our pivot chart by store.

This will update our chart to only include Cardiff and London data.

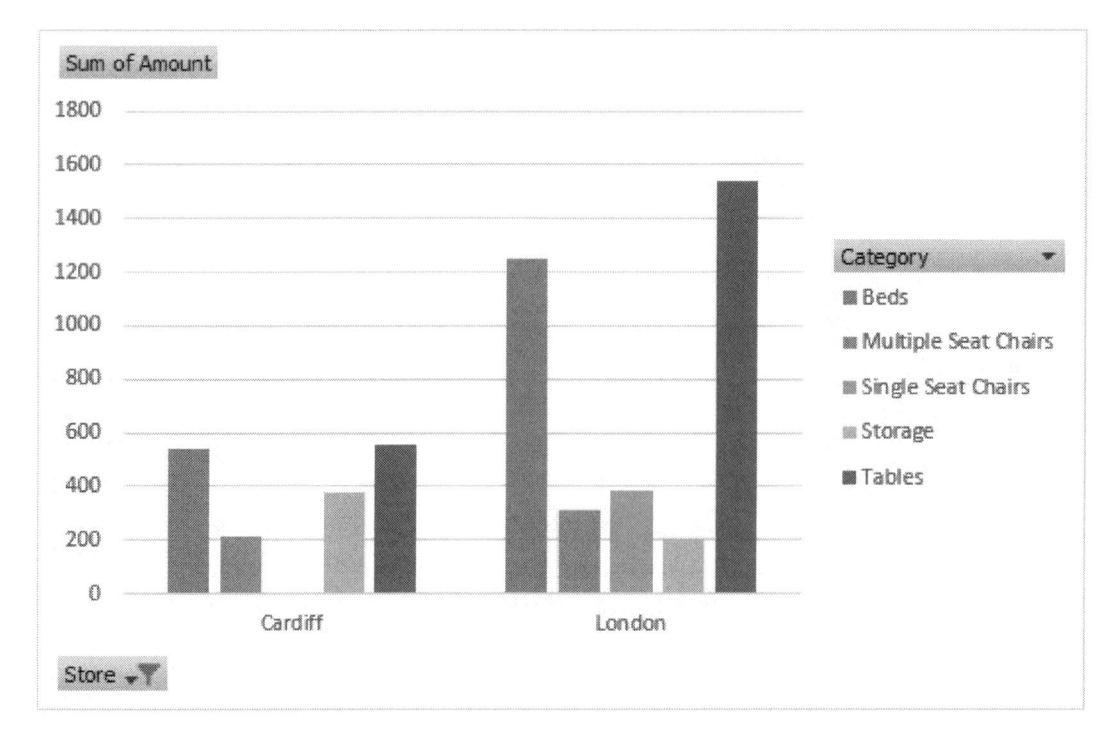

Image 6-6 – Our pivot chart now only shows data for Cardiff and London.

It is worth noting that our pivot table has also been updated to reflect our changes;

Sum of Amount	Column Labels					
Row Labels	Beds	Multiple Seat Chairs	Single Seat Chairs	Storage	Tables	Grand Total
Cardiff	541.36	212.19		374.7	557.18	1685.43
London	1247.57	310.59	387.57	202.6	1539.69	3688.02
Grand Total	1788.93	522.78	387.57	577.3	2096.87	5373.45

Image 6-7 – Our updated pivot table.

We can also filter our data to show selected product categories. In this example, we will select **Multiple Seat Chairs** and **Single Seat Chairs**.

1. Click on the **Category** filter button.

2. Select **Multiple Seat Chairs** and **Single Seat Chairs** from the options available.

3. Click **OK**.

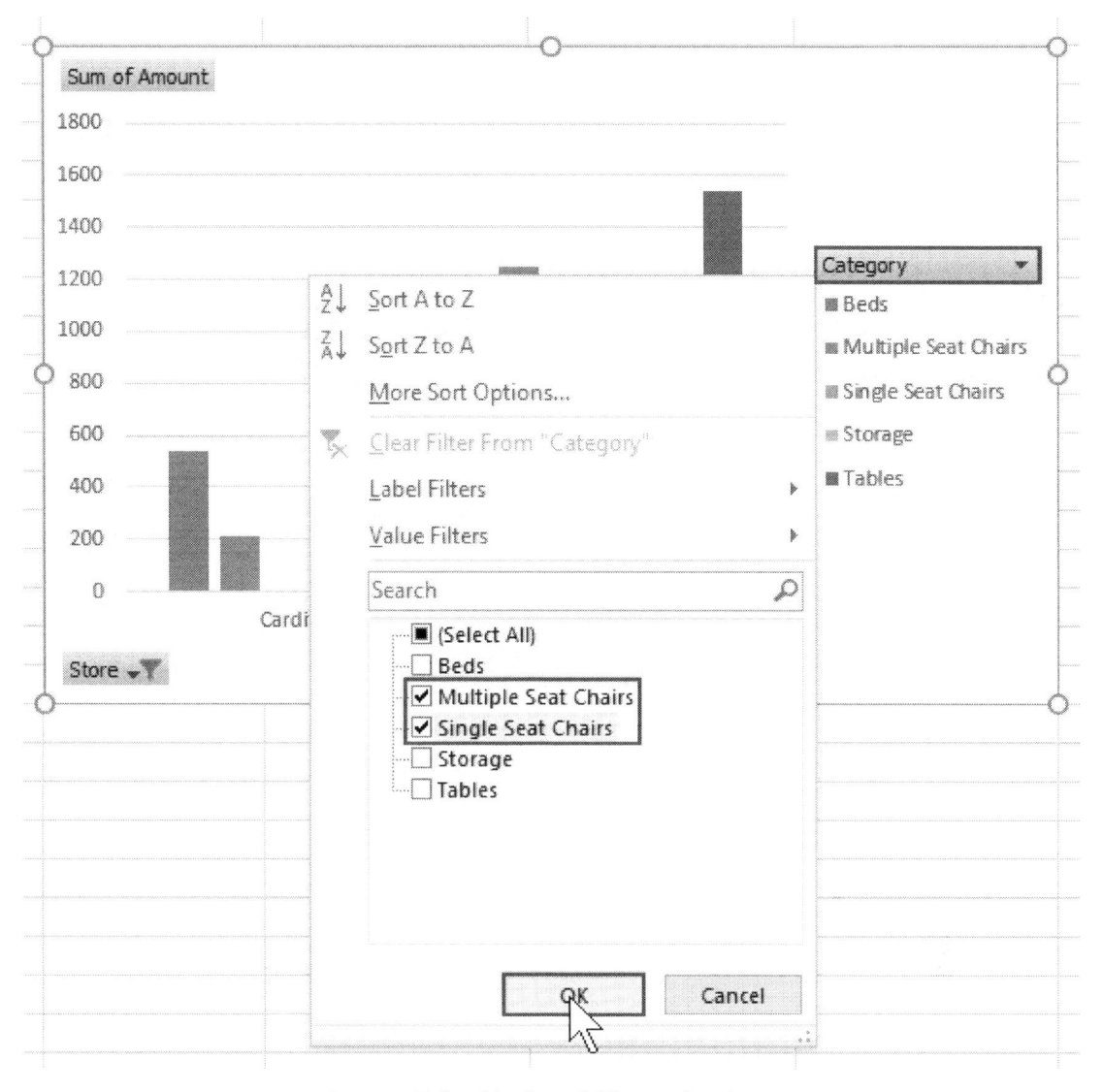

Image 6-8 – Updated filter selections.

This updates our pivot chart to look like this;

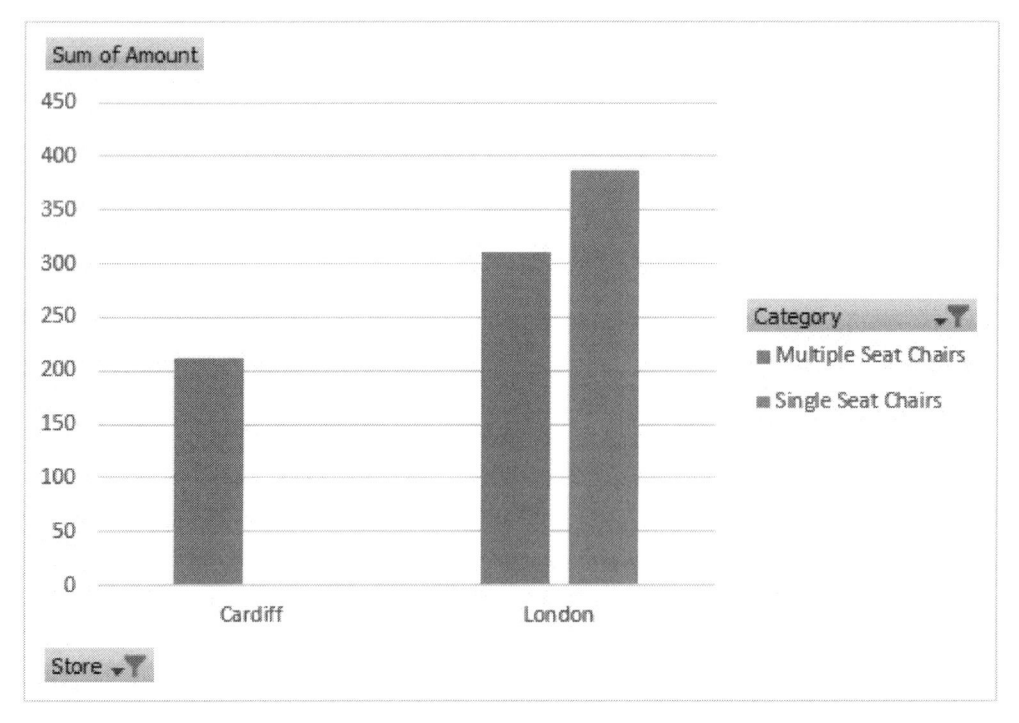

Image 6-9 – Our pivot chart filtered by store and category.

Of course, this also updates our source pivot table.

Sum of Amount	Column Labels		
Row Labels	Multiple Seat Chairs	Single Seat Chairs	Grand Total
Cardiff	212.19		212.19
London	310.59	387.57	698.16
Grand Total	522.78	387.57	910.35

Image 6-10 – Our pivot table filtered by store and category.

It is also worth noting that you can filter and unfilter the chart, using the filters in the pivot table as shown below;

Sum of Amount	Column Labels		
Row Labels	Multiple Seat Chairs	Single Seat Chairs	Grand Total
Cardiff	212.19		212.19
London	310.59	387.57	698.16
Grand Total	**522.78**	**387.57**	**910.35**

Image 6-11 – Alternative filters.

7. Slicing Pivot Tables with Slicers.

Slicers were added to Excel in 2010 and allow for quicker and simpler filtering of pivot tables. They do exactly the same job as the filters we have been using until now, but they are easier to use.

Example Data for Our Pivot Table Slicers.

A copy of the data for this exercise can be found in the **Chapter 7 – Data** tab of the accompanying spreadsheet.

This is what our data looks like;

	A	B	C	D	E	F
1	Order Numb	Product	Category	Store	Date	Amount
2	1	Canopy bed	Beds	Manchester	2016/01/04	£185.94
3	2	Changing table	Tables	Birmingham	2016/01/06	£241.43
4	3	Canopy bed	Beds	Bristol	2016/01/17	£598.31
5	4	Davenport	Multiple Seat Chairs	London	2016/01/24	£310.59
6	5	Changing table	Tables	London	2016/01/26	£151.68
7	6	Bathroom cabinet	Storage	Manchester	2016/02/02	£76.85
8	7	Bunk bed	Beds	Cardiff	2016/02/03	£541.36
9	8	Chest of drawers	Storage	Birmingham	2016/02/08	£122.63
10	9	Bathroom cabinet	Storage	Manchester	2016/02/14	£116.86
11	10	Coat rack	Storage	Swindon	2016/02/17	£139.30
12	12	Daybed	Beds	Manchester	2016/02/21	£149.29

Image 7-1 – The annual sales data from "Sofa, So Good".

And from this data we will produce the two-dimensional pivot table found in the **Chapter 7 – Pivot Table** tab of the example spreadsheet. Refer to **chapter 4** of this tutorial for details on how to build your own two-dimensional pivot table.

Sum of Amount	Column Labels					
Row Labels	Beds	Multiple Seat Chairs	Single Seat Chairs	Storage	Tables	Grand Total
Birmingham	1194.68			661.66	336.21	2192.55
Bristol	1119.09	512.8	306.92	61.93	444.16	2444.9
Cardiff	541.36	212.19		374.7	557.18	1685.43
London	1247.57	310.59	387.57	202.6	1539.69	3688.02
Manchester	899.94	391.73	90.02	349.99		1731.68
Swindon	136.69	349.32	134.8	403.8	761.79	1786.4
Grand Total	5139.33	1776.63	919.31	2054.68	3639.03	13528.98

Image 7-2 – Our two-dimensional pivot table.

Adding A Slicer.

Follow these steps to add a slicer;

1. Click on any cell in the pivot table.

2. This should activate the **PivotTables Tools** section of the Excel ribbon.

3. Click on the **Analyze** sub tab (In older versions of Excel, this sub tab maybe labelled Options).

4. Click on **Insert Slicer**.

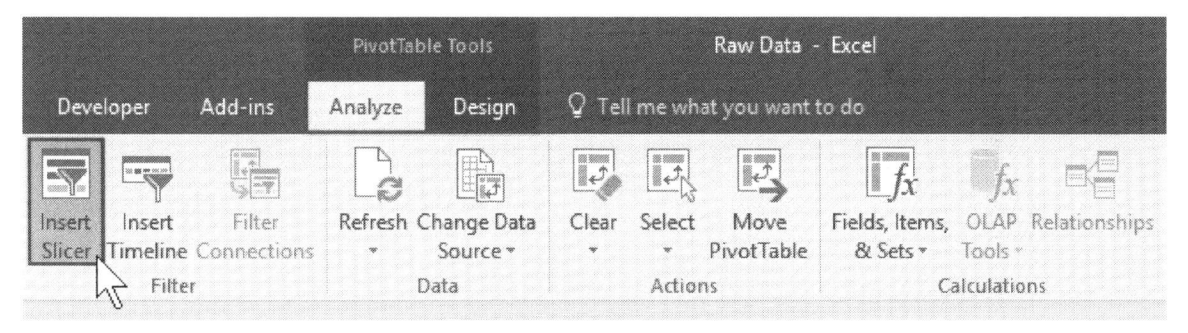

Image 7-3 – Adding a pivot table Slicer.

This will bring up the following **Insert Slicers** form;

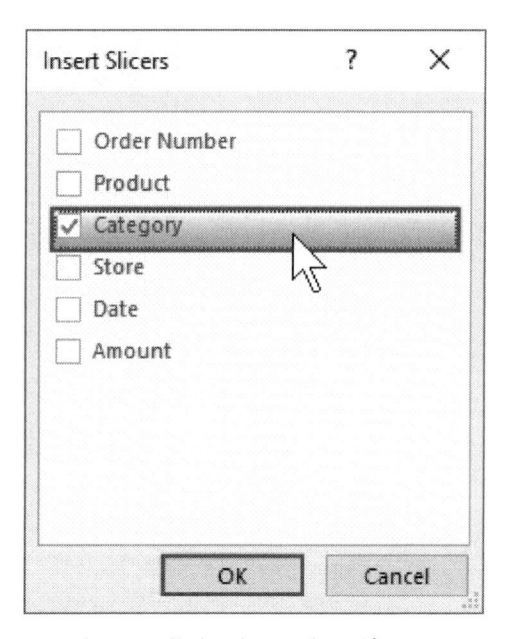

Image 7-4 – Inserting Slicer.

When the window pops up select **Category** and click **OK**.

This will add a slicer filter area to the pivot table sheet.

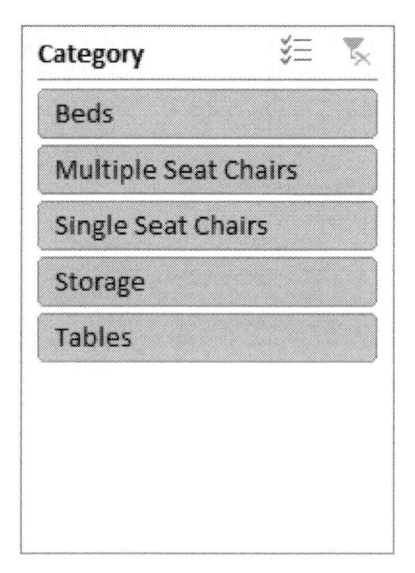

Image 7-5 Slicer filter Area.

If we just want our pivot table to show storage sales, we simply click on the **Storage** button. The Slicer filter area will now look like this;

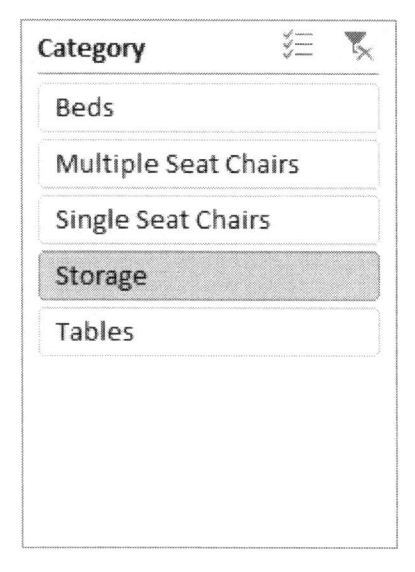

Image 7-6 Filtering by Storage sales.

This in turn will update our pivot to look like this;

Sum of Amount	Column Labels	
Row Labels	Storage	Grand Total
Birmingham	661.66	661.66
Bristol	61.93	61.93
Cardiff	374.7	374.7
London	202.6	202.6
Manchester	349.99	349.99
Swindon	403.8	403.8
Grand Total	**2054.68**	**2054.68**

Image 7-7 Our filtered pivot table.

Note that the filtered symbol appears at the top to show that the table is filtered. Clicking on this shows how the table is filtered.

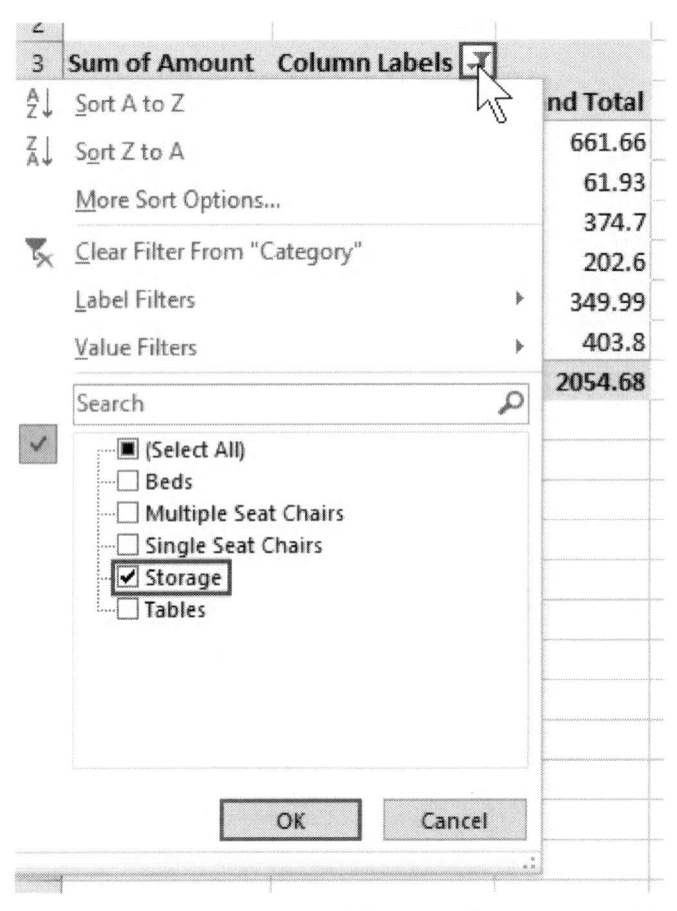

Image 7-8 Clicking on the manual filter confirms we are filtered by storage sales.

Making Multiple Selections.

If we want to make multiple selections, there are two ways of doing this. The method you will use will depend on the selection toggle at the top of the slicer window.

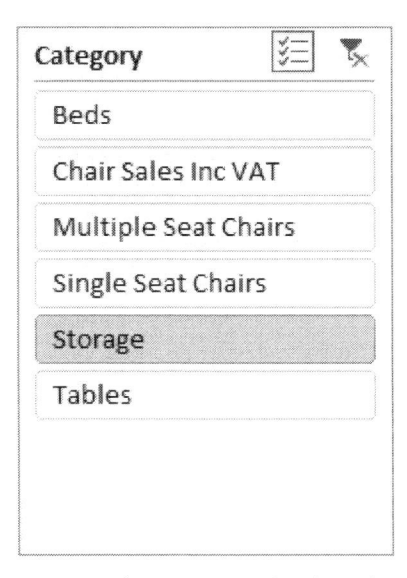

Image 7-9 Making our multiple selections.

When the selection toggle looks like this;

Image 7-10 Multi-select mode.

You can select multiple categories simply by clicking on them. Clicking on each category acts as a toggle and you simply toggle each category on and off. This is probably the easiest mode to make multiple selections in.

When the selection toggle looks like this;

Image 7-11 Single-select mode.

You can only make one selection at a time, however you can override this by holding down the Control Key while you make your multiple selections.

Clearing Your Selections.

If we want to clear our selections, we simply click on the **Clear Filter** button as shown;

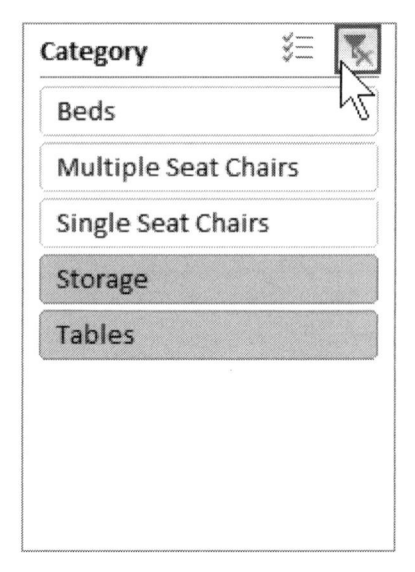

Image 7-12 This will return our pivot table back to an unfiltered table.

8. Updating Pivot Tables.

When you change/update your data it does not automatically update your pivot table. This is probably the biggest downfall of pivot tables. So, when we update our data we have to refresh our pivot tables. Luckily this is a very simple process.

How to Refresh Your Pivot Table.

You simply right click on any cell in your pivot table and select **Refresh**.

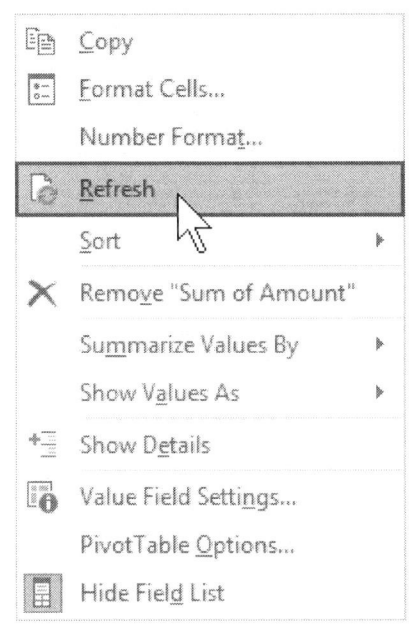

Image 8-1 – Refreshing our pivot table.

How to Handle Large Changes to Your Data.

If you make large changes to your data (e.g. by adding rows or columns) or if you want your pivot table to work on a different set of data, you can redefine your data source.

1. Click on any cell inside your pivot table.

2. Under the **PivotTable Tools** menu select **Analyze** (this will be **Options** in older versions of Excel.

3. Click on **Change Data Source**.

4. Select **Change Data Source**.

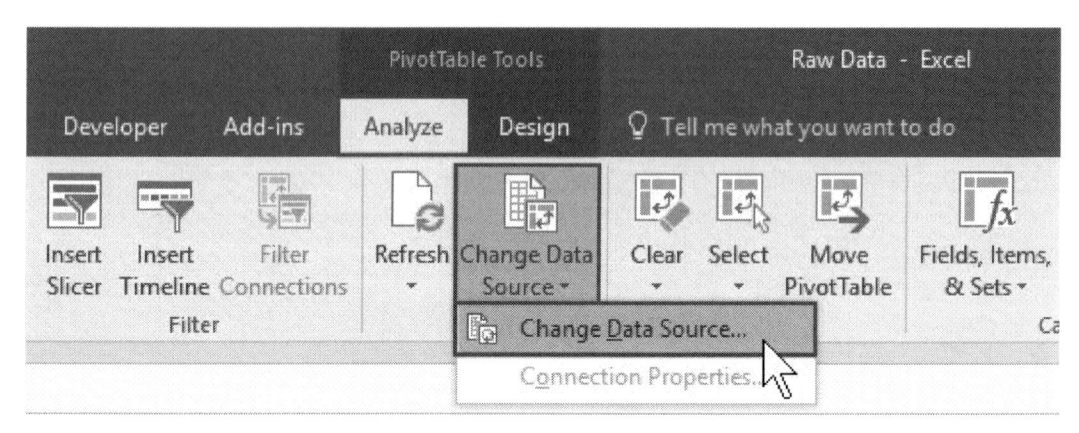

Image 8-2 – Changing our data source.

This will take you back to the pivot tables source data (if it is on another sheet) and allow you to select the new data set with this form.

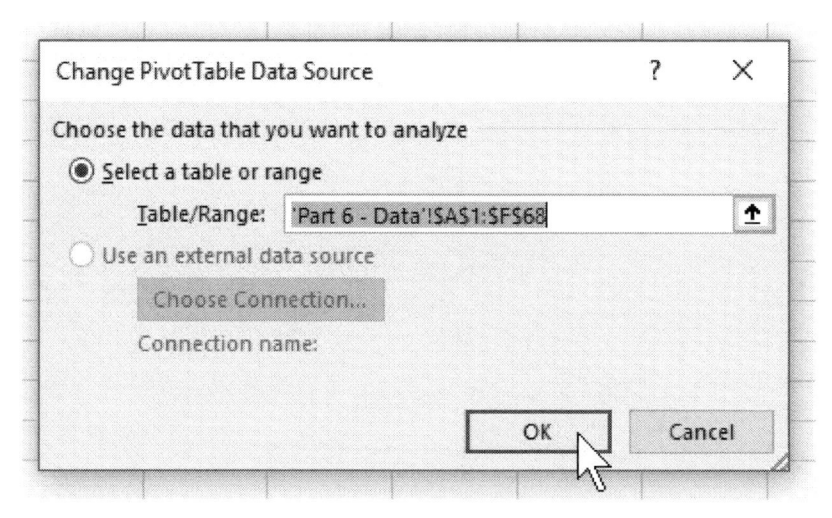

Image 8-3 – Selecting our new data source.

Once you have selected your new data source click on OK.

9. Calculated Fields and Items.

Sometimes we need to use calculations when generating our results. For example, we may need to add VAT (Value Added Tax) or Sales tax.

Example Data for Calculated Fields and Items.

A copy of the data for this exercise can be found in the **Chapter 9 – Data** tab of the accompanying spreadsheet.

This is what our data looks like;

	A	B	C	D	E	F
1	Order Numb	Product	Category	Store	Date	Amount
2	1	Canopy bed	Beds	Manchester	2016/01/04	£185.94
3	2	Changing table	Tables	Birmingham	2016/01/06	£241.43
4	3	Canopy bed	Beds	Bristol	2016/01/17	£598.31
5	4	Davenport	Multiple Seat Chairs	London	2016/01/24	£310.59
6	5	Changing table	Tables	London	2016/01/26	£151.68
7	6	Bathroom cabinet	Storage	Manchester	2016/02/02	£76.85
8	7	Bunk bed	Beds	Cardiff	2016/02/03	£541.36
9	8	Chest of drawers	Storage	Birmingham	2016/02/08	£122.63
10	9	Bathroom cabinet	Storage	Manchester	2016/02/14	£116.86
11	10	Coat rack	Storage	Swindon	2016/02/17	£139.30
12	12	Daybed	Beds	Manchester	2016/02/21	£149.29

Image 9-1 – The annual sales data from "Sofa, So Good".

And from this data we will produce the pivot table found in the **Chapter 9 – Pivot Table** tab of the accompanying spreadsheet. This pivot table breaks the sales figures down by product type.

Row Labels	Sum of Amount
Beds	5139.33
Multiple Seat Chairs	1776.63
Single Seat Chairs	919.31
Storage	2054.68
Tables	3639.03
Grand Total	**13528.98**

Image 9-2 – Our sales pivot table breaking sales down by product type.

Adding A Calculated Field.

A calculated field is one that applies a calculation to a field to produce a new field. For example, a calculated field to include sales tax would use the sales field as the basis for the calculation. To add a calculated field, follow these steps;

1. Click on any cell in the pivot table to activate the **Pivot Table Tools** section of the main Excel ribbon menu.

2. Select the **Analyze** (**Options** in older versions of Excel) sub menu.

3. Click **Fields, Items & Sets.**

4. Click **Calculated Fields…**

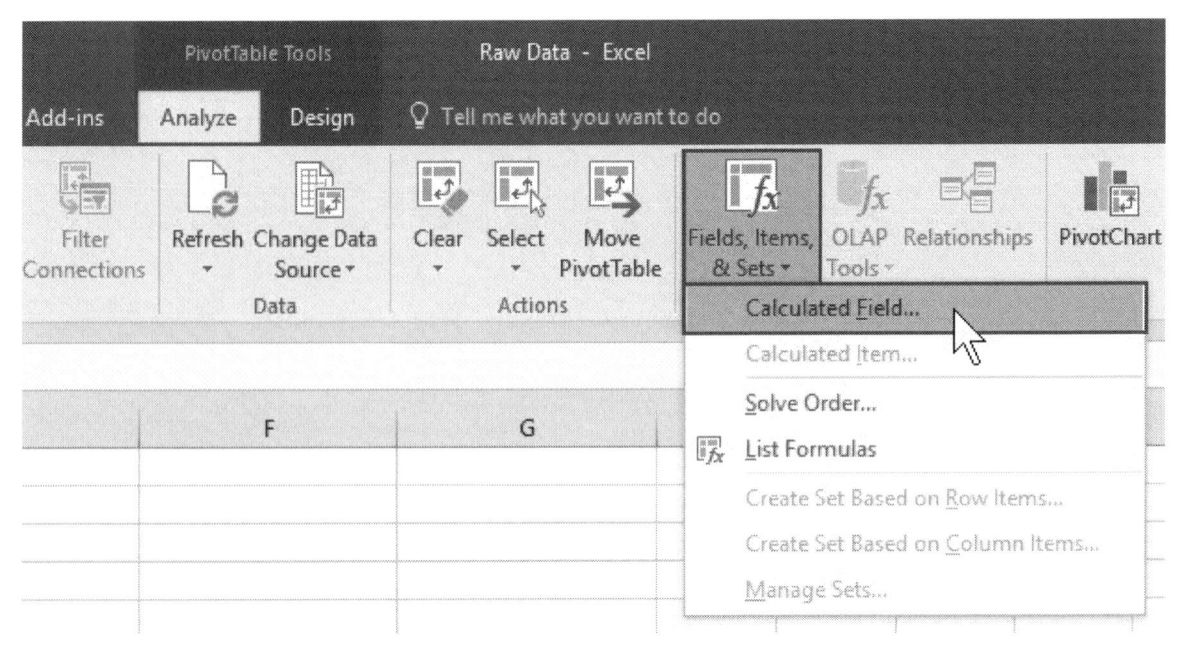

Image 9-3 – Selecting Calculated Fields.

This will bring up the **Insert Calculated Field** window;

Image 9-4 – The Insert Calculated Field window.

In this exercise, we are going to add VAT (the UK version of Sales Tax) to our figures. At the time of putting this tutorial together VAT stands at 20%. We achieve this by setting the following settings;

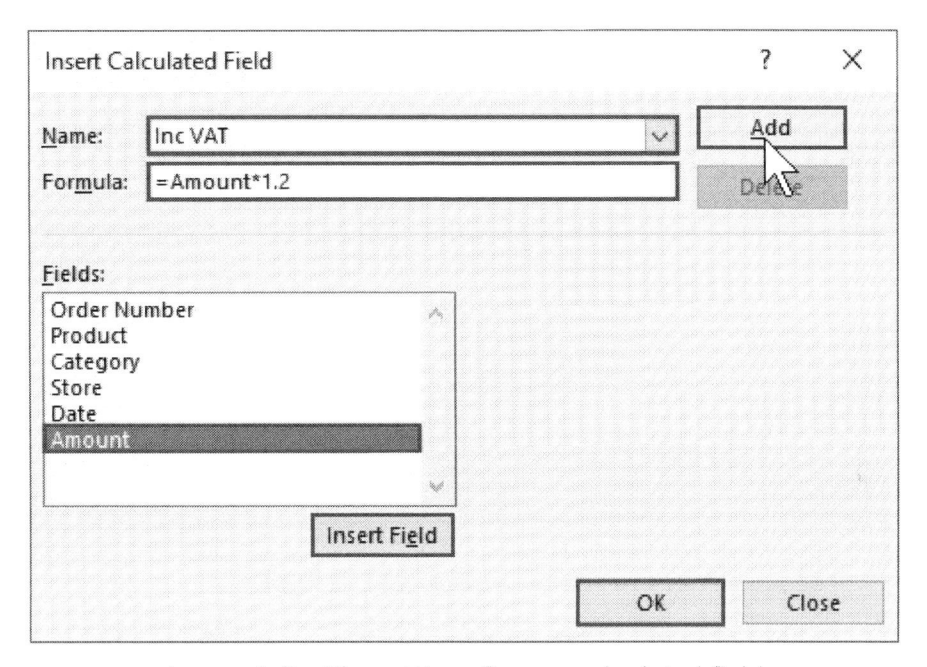

Image 9-5 – The settings for our calculated field.

1. In the **Name:** field enter the name for your new field – in our example we are calling it "Inc VAT".

2. In the **Fields:** area click on **Amount**.

3. Click on the **Insert Field** button.

4. The **Formula:** field should now read **=Amount**

5. Add ***1.2** to the **Formula:** field so it reads **=Amount*1.2**

6. Click the **Add** button.

7. Click the **OK** button.

This will add a new column to our pivot table to make it look like this;

Row Labels	Sum of Amount	Sum of Inc VAT
Beds	5139.33	£6,167.20
Multiple Seat Chairs	1776.63	£2,131.96
Single Seat Chairs	919.31	£1,103.17
Storage	2054.68	£2,465.62
Tables	3639.03	£4,366.84
Grand Total	13528.98	£16,234.78

Image 9-6 – The calculated field added to our pivot table.

Adding A Calculated Item.

Adding a calculated item calculates a single item/result from other single items. In this example, we are going to calculate the sales of chairs (multiple seat and single seat combined) including VAT (sales tax).

Follow these steps to achieve this;

Row Labels	Sum of Amount
Beds	5139.33
Multiple Seat Chairs	1776.63
Single Seat Chairs	919.31
Storage	2054.68
Tables	3639.03
Grand Total	13528.98

Image 9-7 – Important – Select one of these cells only.

1. Select one of the category names in the pivot table. If you select the amounts or the headings this process will not work.

2. Select the **Analyze (Options** in older versions of Excel) sub menu.

3. Click **Fields, Items & Sets**.

4. Click **Calculated Item...** (If you clicked on anything other than a product type in step 1, this option will be greyed out).

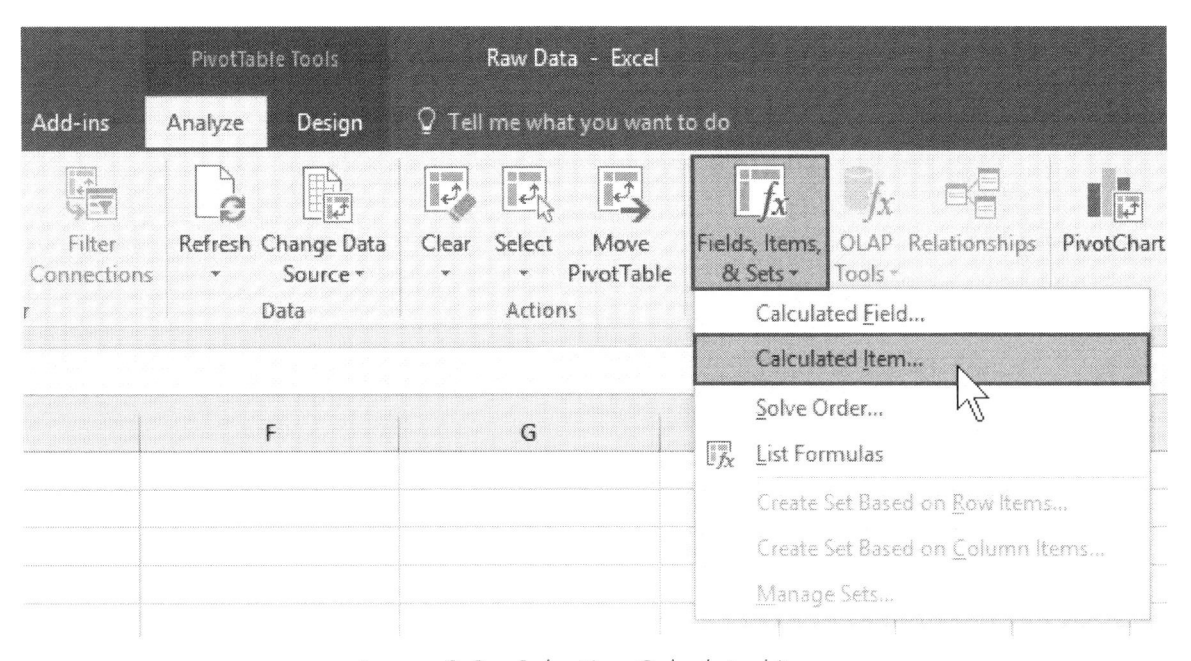

Image 9-8 – Selecting Calculated Item.

This will bring up the Insert Calculated Item window;

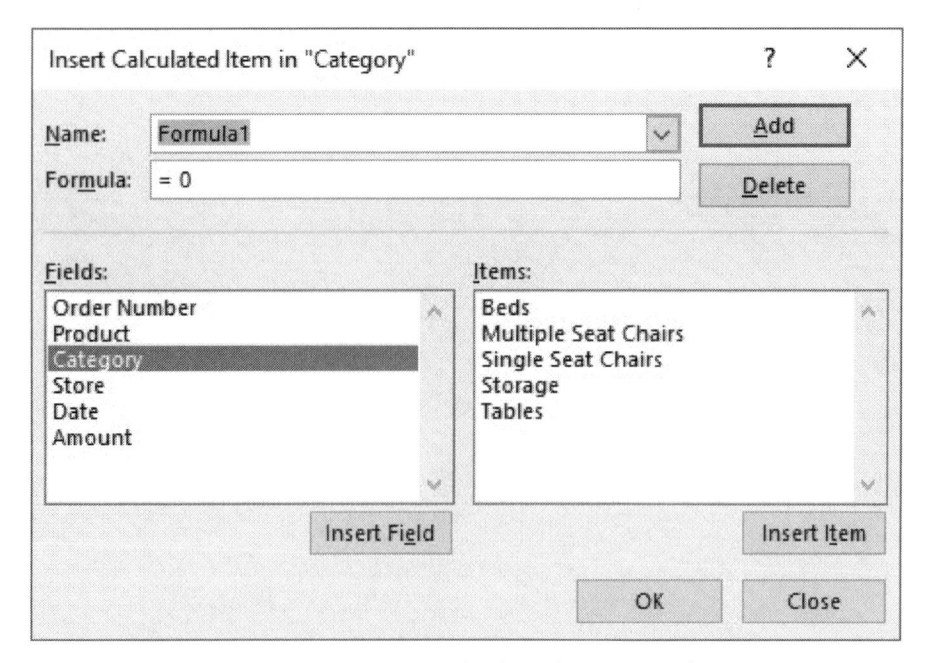

Image 9-9 – Insert Calculated Item window.

To combine the Multiple Seat Chairs and Single Seat Chairs with VAT (Sales Tax) we enter the following settings;

1. In the **Name:** field enter the name of the desired item. In our example, we will call it "Chair Sales Inc VAT".

2. Enter =(in the Formula: field.

3. In the **Items:** field click on **Multiple Seat Chairs** and then the **Insert Item** button.

4. The **Formula:** field should now read =('Multiple Seat Chairs'

5. Add a **+** to the end of the formula so it reads =('Multiple Seat Chairs'+

6. In the **Items:** field click on **Single Seat Chairs** and then the **Insert Item** button.

7. The **Formula:** field should now read =('Multiple Seat Chairs'+'Single Seat Chairs'

8. Add a **)** to the end of the formula so it reads =('Multiple Seat Chairs'+ Single Seat Chairs')

9. Click **OK**.

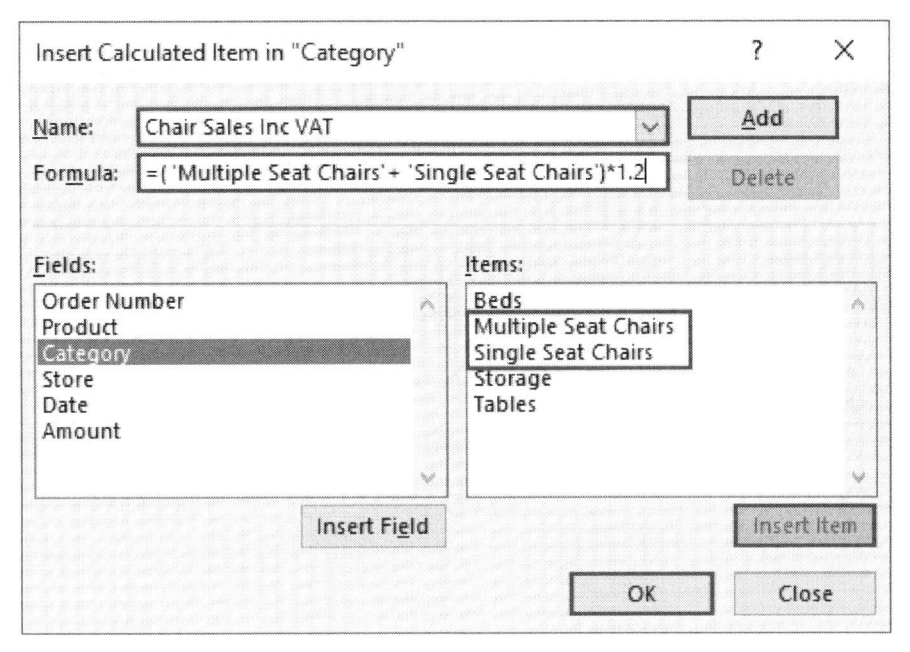

Image 9-10 – The settings for our calculated item.

Our pivot table will now include a **Chair Sales Inc VAT** field.

Row Labels	Sum of Amount
Beds	5139.33
Multiple Seat Chairs	1776.63
Single Seat Chairs	919.31
Storage	2054.68
Tables	3639.03
Chair Sales Inc VAT	3235.128
Grand Total	**16764.108**

Image 9-11 – Our calculated item added to our pivot table.

Try Our Other Books

Available on Amazon or get more details from our website;

www.Excel-Expert.com

Excel-Expert
Making Excel Easy

Printed in Great Britain
by Amazon